COLORS & MARKINGS OF THE
EA-6B
PROWLER

in detail & scale

Bert Kinzey

squadron/signal publications

COPYRIGHT 1994 BY DETAIL & SCALE, INC.

This book is a product of Detail & Scale, Inc., which has sole responsibility for its content and layout, except that all contributors are responsible for the security clearance and copyright release of all materials submitted. Published by Squadron/Signal Publications, 1115 Crowley Drive, Carrollton, TX 75011. ISBN 1-888974-22-2.

CONTRIBUTORS AND SOURCES:

LCDR Fred Drummond, USN
LT David D'Muro, USN
Jim Rotramel
Dana Bell
Mick Roth
Wayne Wachsmuth
Alan Toon

Joe Driver, Jr.
Clyde Mills
Bobby Winnett
Walt Holmes
Flightleader
Lois Lovisolo, Grumman History Center
NAS Oceana, Virginia, Public Affairs Office

USS JOHN F. KENNEDY, CV-67, Public Affairs Office
USS EISENHOWER, CVN-69, Public Affairs Office
COMNAVAIRLANT Public Affairs Office
VAQ-130 "Zappers"
U. S. Navy
U. S. Marine Corps
Department of Defense

Many photographs in this publication are credited to their contributors. Photographs with no credit indicated were taken by the author.

A very special word of thanks goes to Lois Lovisolo at Grumman. Over the years, Lois has been very helpful during the preparation of at least a dozen Detail & Scale books, and she is well known among aviation authors and researchers for her efforts and abilities in finding just what is needed for anyone who had a request for photographs, drawings, and information. Realizing the importance of aviation history, Lois always went far beyond the call of duty when it came to making Grumman's files available to everyone who had a need for access to them. As this is written, the excellent Grumman History Center is being closed as the company merges with Northrop. Efforts are being made to retain the History Center's files somewhere on Long Island, but the results of these efforts are not yet known. But regardless of what happens, the days of working with Lois are sadly over, and she will be missed by everyone she has ever helped.

Front cover; EA-6B, 158800, is painted in the early colors of VAQ-138 and Carrier Air Wing One while assigned to the USS JOHN F. KENNEDY, CV-67. CDR Ed O'Neal was the first squardon commander of VAQ-138, and because he was a Georgia Tech graduate, he named the squadron the "Yellow Jackets" in honor of his alma mater. A yellow jacket is painted on the tail of the aircraft to denote the squardon's nickname. (Grumman)

Rear cover, top: Colors and details of the instrument panel in the front cockpit of an ICAP-1 EA-6B are revealed in this factory photograph. Note the hole in the right side where the panel for the ALQ-149 system was supposed to be installed. However, the system was cancelled, thus leaving a hole in the instrument panel. (Grumman)

Rear cover, bottom: This is the instrument panel in the rear cockpit of an ICAP-1 EA-6B. (Grumman)

INTRODUCTION

From the front, the Prowler looks anything but aerodynamic. Note the offset refueling probe and the stylized nose marking. Prowlers almost always carry some sort of nose marking to assist LSOs in distinguishing them from Intruders during daylight landings aboard ship. For night landings, the lights on the aft end of the inboard wing pylons on Prowlers are green on the right and red on the left. Both lights are amber on Intruders. The glow cast on the lowered trailing edge flaps by the lights tells the LSO which type of aircraft is approaching the ship. (Sides via Flightleader)

Adapted from the airframe of Grumman's highly successful A-6 Intruder, the EA-6B Prowler first saw combat during the closing months of the war in Vietnam. Since then, the Prowler has flown vital missions to protect Navy carrier-based aircraft every time they have gone into combat against enemy ground forces. During Operation Desert Storm, Navy and Marine Prowlers not only jammed Iraqi radars and communications to protect coalition aircraft, they also fired AGM-88 HARM anti-radiation missiles to destroy hostile radar sites. In spite of the fact that these missions are among the most dangerous assigned to any aircraft, no EA-6B has ever been lost in combat.

The Prowler has now been in service for more than twenty years, and current plans call for it to remain operational well into the twenty-first century. Over the years, constant upgrades have been made to the aircraft in order to keep it current with the ever changing threat. Although no changes have been made to the EA-6B designation, the Prowler has been improved dramatically since it originally entered service in 1971. Acronyms, including EXCAP, ICAP-1, and ICAP-2, have all been used to identify the ongoing improvements made to the aircraft. Subvariants of ICAP-2 Prowlers are known as Block 82, Block 86, and Block 89 aircraft. This new publication in the Detail & Scale Series explains these improvements, and more importantly, it illustrates the physical changes associated with each through the use of drawings and detailed photographs.

One of the highlights of this book is the historical summary written by LCDR Fred Drummond who has flown over 1500 hours as an electronic countermeasures officer (ECMO) in the EA-6B. LCDR Drummond flew combat missions in the Prowler during the raids against Libya in 1986, against Iran in the Gulf of Sidra during 1988, and again in Operation Southern Watch against Iraq in 1993. During Operation Desert Storm, (then) LT Drummond was

on exchange duty with the U. S. Air Force, and he flew combat missions in the EF-111A Raven. Today, he remains the only person ever to experience combat in both aircraft. This makes him uniquely qualified to compare the capabilities and limitations of each, and his interesting narrative provides unique insight into the operational use of Prowler and the Raven which is not available anywhere else.

As is the case with all books in the Detail & Scale Series, the main focus of this publication is the many physical details of the aircraft. Scores of detailed photographs are included, and almost all of them were taken specifically for this publication. They reveal the Prowler's details, features, and updates more extensively than any other reference. Captions carefully explain what is being illustrated and point out differences between the various Prowler upgrades and to the basic Intruder design. In special cases, detailed photographs of the Intruder are also included as a comparison in order to illustrate the not-so-obvious changes made to the airframe. Some of these differences have never been shown before in any other publication.

Five-view drawings have been produced specifically for this publication by noted aviation researcher Dana Bell, and they are in the popular 1/72nd modeling scale.

Also included are a few pages on the EA-6A Electric Intruder. A photographic "walk-around" illustrates many of the important details of this aircraft.

The modelers section at the end of this book provides informative and objective reviews of EA-6A and EA-6B kits that are available to the serious scale modeler, and it also includes a listing of available after-market decals.

This publication would not have been possible without the efforts and assistance provided by the contributors listed on page 2. To all of them, and especially to LCDR Drummond, the author expresses a sincere word of thanks.

HISTORICAL SUMMARY

One of the five Prowler prototypes, known as development aircraft, is shown here with a long instrumentation boom attached to its radome. Barely visible is a wire antenna trailing from the base of the "football" atop the vertical tail. Unlike production Prowlers, this development aircraft has the metal wing originally used on Intruders. As will be illustrated in this book, the wing used on production Prowlers was considerably different from both the metal and composite wings used on Intruders. Also note the lack of an HF antenna fairing on the spine of the aircraft. Development EA-6Bs were delivered to the Navy between April 1968 and March 1970. Bureau numbers for these aircraft were from 156478 to 156482.   *(Grumman)*

LCDR Fred Drummond graduated from Virginia Tech in 1983 with a BA in English. He then received his commission through Aviation Officer Candidate School at Pensacola, Florida, in July 1983. After completing ECMO training in VAQ-129, his initial assignment was to VAQ-135 where he served in ICAP Prowlers between 1985-1988. Fred flew combat missions in the EA-6B during Operations El Dorado Canyon (Libya, 1986) and Praying Mantis (Arabian Gulf, 1988). In 1988, he was assigned to Mountain Home AFB, Idaho, for an exchange tour in EF-111A Ravens with the U. S. Air Force. This tour lasted until after the Gulf War in 1991, so this gave Fred the opportunity to fly combat missions in the EF-111A during Operation Desert Storm. He also flew additional missions in Operation Just Cause. He returned to ICAP-2 Prowlers late in 1991, and spent sixteen months in VAQ-134. While assigned to VAQ-134, Fred participated in the strikes against Iraq in January 1993.

LCDR Drummond has written the Historical Summary for this book and has provided an unusual personal perspective. He not only reviews and explains the development of the Prowler and its various upgrades, he recounts the EA-6B's use in combat with the insight of someone who has actually participated in those missions. As the only person to have ever flown combat missions in both the EA-6B Prowler and the EF-111A Raven, he is uniquely

qualified to compare the capabilities of these two aircraft. In his narrative, Fred explains the strengths and weaknesses of both aircraft and their systems.

LCDR Drummond is currently assigned to VAQ-130.

Prowler Development

The EA-6B flying today is the fourth major version of the Prowler. From its first operational use with the EA-6B training squadron in late 1970 until the recent cancellation of the ADVCAP version, the Prowler has undergone a steady series of significant configuration improvements. The four versions are: Standard, EXCAP, ICAP-1, and ICAP-2. As of this writing there are three subvariants of ICAP-2, which are called Block 82, Block 86, and Block 89 for the fiscal year in which they were approved.

The first three Prowlers were rebuilds of the numbers 5, 15, and 16 A-6As. One of these three was a non-flying Electronics Test Article, or ETA. The other two were NEA-6Bs used for initial flight testing. All three were accepted by the Navy in 1968. Five pre-production EA-6Bs followed in 1969-1970.

The first Standard aircraft (also referred to as Basic in Navy publications) was accepted in January 1971. As the baseline for all future Prowlers, the Standard's ALQ-99 Tactical Jamming System (TJS) had only four frequency bands with limited jamming modes. The crew of four has always consisted of a pilot and three Electronic CounterMeasures Officers (ECMOs). Crew stationing includes the pilot in the left front seat, ECMO-1 in the right front, ECMO-2 in the right rear, and ECMO-3 behind the pilot. In the Standard Prowlers, Electronic Warfare (EW) duties were split between ECMO-1 and ECMO-2, with the ECMO-3 operating the ALQ-92 communications jammer. A total of twenty-three Standard Prowlers were built, and the last operational use of this version was in 1977.

EXCAP, for EXpanded CAPability, was introduced in January 1973, and featured greater frequency coverage

EA-6B, 158033, was the fifth of twenty-three Prowlers built to the Standard configuration. These aircraft were delivered from January 1971 to November 1972, and all were later upgraded to ICAP standards. This aircraft carries the markings of the "Scorpions" of VAQ-132. *(Grumman)*

for the receivers and jammers. It also had additional computer memory, and a more complex jamming mode was added. The crew responsibilities were the same as in the Standard aircraft. EXCAP upgraded the ALQ-99 system to the ALQ-99B and C versions. EXCAP production was twenty-five aircraft, and these were flown until March of 1985. Standard and EXCAP aircraft looked the same externally, and could be identified from later versions by the ALQ-100 Defensive Electronic CounterMeasures (DECM) antennas that were attached to the leading edges of the number 1 and 5 pylons.

Even as EXCAP was being introduced to the fleet, the ICAP version, for Improved CAPability, was under development. The first ICAP, later called ICAP-1 when ICAP-2 came about, was accepted in March, 1976. ICAP's ALQ-99D resulted in wholesale improvements to the entire Tactical Jamming System (TJS), and included digital receivers and new displays. A new cockpit arrangement was also introduced, with all of the ALQ-99 operations now being carried out in the rear cockpit by ECMOs 2 and 3. This cockpit rearrangement improved crew efficiency with ECMO-1 becoming a full-time navigator, assisting in co-pilot duties, and operating the ALQ-92. This cockpit set-up remains the same in today's Prowlers. As an aside, the EF-111A's ALQ-99E is comparable to early versions of the Prowler's ALQ-99D. The only exception is the addition of the jamming subsystem's universal

exciter which did not reach the Prowler until ICAP-2.

There were forty-five new production ICAP-1 aircraft, and twenty Standard aircraft were also upgraded to ICAP-1 standards. All were out of operational use by 1989. ICAP-1 aircraft incorporated the ALQ-126 DECM equipment for self-protection. The two antenna housings for the ALQ-126 include the protrusion or "saw tooth" at the bottom of the refueling probe and the "beer can" at the bottom of the tail fin radome or "football." Some ICAP-1 aircraft had the ALQ-92 communications jammer installed, but these were gone from the fleet before 1985. Many aircraft still had the ALQ-92 antenna directly in front of the nose gear even after the removal of the equipment. In addition, an interim communications jammer was used by many squadrons on deployments aboard west coast aircraft carriers.

ICAP-1 aircraft can be distinguished from ICAP-2 by the radome on the bottom of the aft fuselage just in front of the tail hook. This radome was for the Doppler navigation radar. ICAP-2 deleted the Doppler radar and its radome, and it also deleted the ALQ-92 cooling scoop on the upper aft fuselage on the port side.

The first ICAP-2 aircraft was introduced in January 1984. ICAP-2's ALQ-99F incorporated a new mission computer, new displays, loading of EW and navigation data by cartridge tape, an increased number of complex jamming modes, and an increase in frequency coverage.

EA-6B, 160791, was one of forty-five Prowlers originally produced as an ICAP-1 aircraft. These aircraft were delivered between March 1976 and November 1983. Note the addition of the "beer can" antenna on the aft end of the "football" fairing at the top of the vertical tail and the sawtooth antenna at the base of the refueling probe. Both of these antennas were associated with the ALQ-126 system. This aircraft has markings belonging to the "Zappers" of VAQ-130 while the squadron was assigned to the USS FORRESTAL, CV-59. *(Grumman)*

EA-6B MAIN DIFFERENCES DRAWINGS

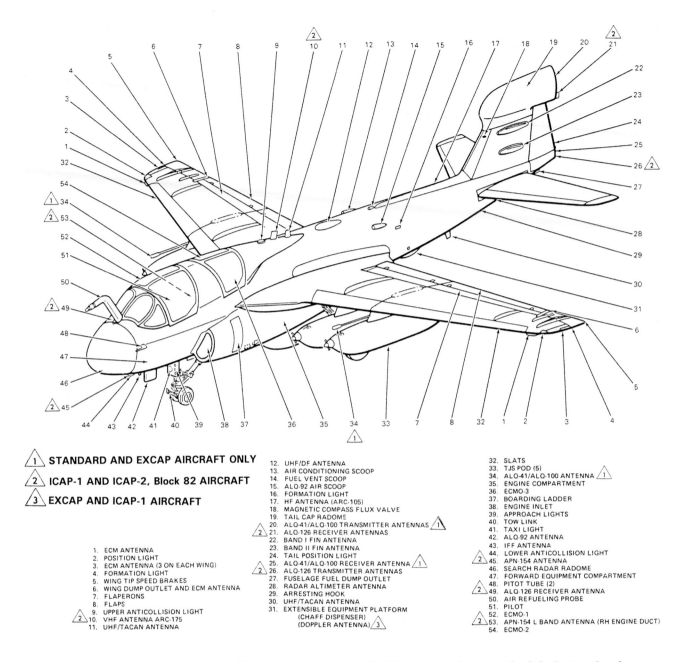

△1 **STANDARD AND EXCAP AIRCRAFT ONLY**

△2 **ICAP-1 AND ICAP-2, Block 82 AIRCRAFT**

△3 **EXCAP AND ICAP-1 AIRCRAFT**

1. ECM ANTENNA
2. POSITION LIGHT
3. ECM ANTENNA (3 ON EACH WING)
4. FORMATION LIGHT
5. WING TIP SPEED BRAKES
6. WING DUMP OUTLET AND ECM ANTENNA
7. FLAPERONS
8. FLAPS
9. UPPER ANTICOLLISION LIGHT
10. VHF ANTENNA ARC-175 △2
11. UHF/TACAN ANTENNA

12. UHF/DF ANTENNA
13. AIR CONDITIONING SCOOP
14. FUEL VENT SCOOP
15. ALQ-92 AIR SCOOP
16. FORMATION LIGHT
17. HF ANTENNA (ARC-105)
18. MAGNETIC COMPASS FLUX VALVE
19. TAIL CAP RADOME
20. ALQ-41/ALQ-100 TRANSMITTER ANTENNAS △1
21. ALQ-126 RECEIVER ANTENNAS △2
22. BAND I FIN ANTENNA
23. BAND II FIN ANTENNA
24. TAIL POSITION LIGHT
25. ALQ-41/ALQ-100 RECEIVER ANTENNA △1
26. ALQ-126 TRANSMITTER ANTENNAS △2
27. FUSELAGE FUEL DUMP OUTLET
28. RADAR ALTIMETER ANTENNA
29. ARRESTING HOOK
30. UHF/TACAN ANTENNA
31. EXTENSIBLE EQUIPMENT PLATFORM
    (CHAFF DISPENSER)
    (DOPPLER ANTENNA) △3

32. SLATS
33. TJS POD (5)
34. ALQ-41/ALQ-100 ANTENNA △1
35. ENGINE COMPARTMENT
36. ECMO-3
37. BOARDING LADDER
38. ENGINE INLET
39. APPROACH LIGHTS
40. TOW LINK
41. TAXI LIGHT
42. ALQ-92 ANTENNA
43. IFF ANTENNA
44. LOWER ANTICOLLISION LIGHT
45. APN-154 ANTENNA △2
46. SEARCH RADAR RADOME
47. FORWARD EQUIPMENT COMPARTMENT
48. PITOT TUBE (2)
49. ALQ-126 RECEIVER ANTENNA △2
50. AIR REFUELING PROBE
51. PILOT
52. ECMO-1
53. APN-154 L BAND ANTENNA (RH ENGINE DUCT) △2
54. ECMO-2

This general arrangement drawing identifies the features of the EA-6B, but more importantly, it indicates the changes in features between the various upgrades of the aircraft up to the ICAP-2, Block 82 version. It should be noted that the external physical features of the Standard and EXCAP aircraft were essentially the same. (U. S. Navy)

Also introduced was an inertial navigation system in place of the old Doppler navigation system. TEAMS, the EA-6B Mission planning System, was another new item. TEAMS allows complete EW mission planning that loads all the ALQ-99 data onto cartridge tapes which are then used to load the aircraft's mission computer. Extensive pre-flight planning and analysis are conducted by the ECMOs on TEAMS, and mission data recorded during flight can be replayed and analyzed for post-flight evaluation.

In 1988, a sub-variant of ICAP-2 was introduced. Normally just called Block 86, this version has a minor modification to a part of the ALQ-99 system, but it added full HARM integration to the Prowler and also incorporated some radio upgrades. The original ICAP-2s are now known as Block 82, although many people incorrectly use

the term ICAP-2 exclusively when referring to this version. To further confuse the picture, fleet Block 86 aircraft began modification to Block 89 standards in 1994. Block 89 mods include aircraft and safety improvements with no external changes. Block 82 and Block 86/89 aircraft have minor differences in external antennas. In 1994, a new interim communications jammer, the USQ-113, was being installed in many fleet aircraft. The key distinguishing feature of this addition is a large radome covering a blade antenna on the extensible equipment platform or "birdcage." This is located on the bottom of the aircraft just forward of the tail hook.

Block 82 production totalled thirty-five new aircraft. Block 86 new production was thirty-six aircraft, and there was one newly built Block 89 Prowler. In addition, surviv-

BLOCK 86 FEATURES

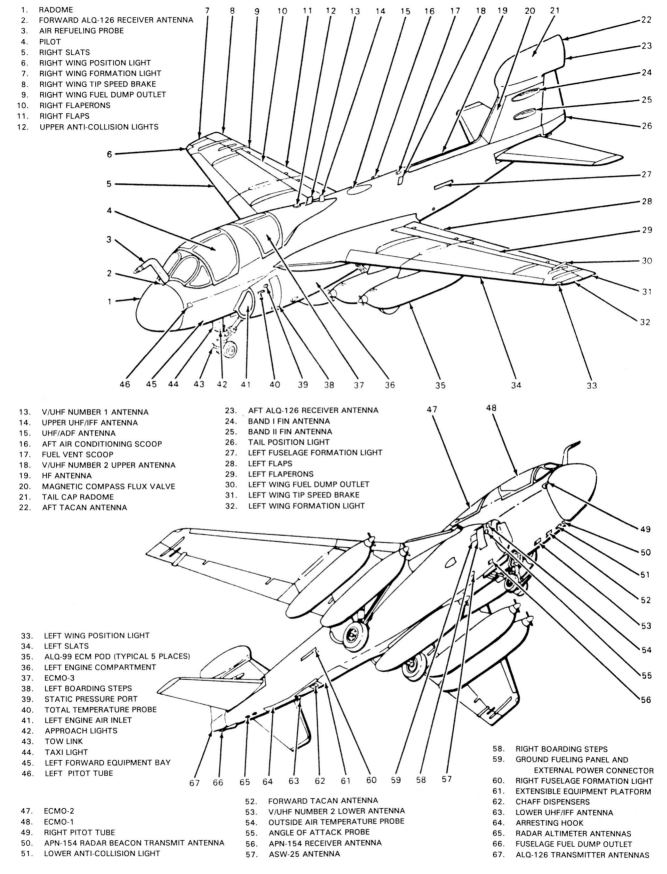

1. RADOME
2. FORWARD ALQ-126 RECEIVER ANTENNA
3. AIR REFUELING PROBE
4. PILOT
5. RIGHT SLATS
6. RIGHT WING POSITION LIGHT
7. RIGHT WING FORMATION LIGHT
8. RIGHT WING TIP SPEED BRAKE
9. RIGHT WING FUEL DUMP OUTLET
10. RIGHT FLAPERONS
11. RIGHT FLAPS
12. UPPER ANTI-COLLISION LIGHTS

13. V/UHF NUMBER 1 ANTENNA
14. UPPER UHF/IFF ANTENNA
15. UHF/ADF ANTENNA
16. AFT AIR CONDITIONING SCOOP
17. FUEL VENT SCOOP
18. V/UHF NUMBER 2 UPPER ANTENNA
19. HF ANTENNA
20. MAGNETIC COMPASS FLUX VALVE
21. TAIL CAP RADOME
22. AFT TACAN ANTENNA

23. AFT ALQ-126 RECEIVER ANTENNA
24. BAND I FIN ANTENNA
25. BAND II FIN ANTENNA
26. TAIL POSITION LIGHT
27. LEFT FUSELAGE FORMATION LIGHT
28. LEFT FLAPS
29. LEFT FLAPERONS
30. LEFT WING FUEL DUMP OUTLET
31. LEFT WING TIP SPEED BRAKE
32. LEFT WING FORMATION LIGHT

33. LEFT WING POSITION LIGHT
34. LEFT SLATS
35. ALQ-99 ECM POD (TYPICAL 5 PLACES)
36. LEFT ENGINE COMPARTMENT
37. ECMO-3
38. LEFT BOARDING STEPS
39. STATIC PRESSURE PORT
40. TOTAL TEMPERATURE PROBE
41. LEFT ENGINE AIR INLET
42. APPROACH LIGHTS
43. TOW LINK
44. TAXI LIGHT
45. LEFT FORWARD EQUIPMENT BAY
46. LEFT PITOT TUBE

47. ECMO-2
48. ECMO-1
49. RIGHT PITOT TUBE
50. APN-154 RADAR BEACON TRANSMIT ANTENNA
51. LOWER ANTI-COLLISION LIGHT

52. FORWARD TACAN ANTENNA
53. V/UHF NUMBER 2 LOWER ANTENNA
54. OUTSIDE AIR TEMPERATURE PROBE
55. ANGLE OF ATTACK PROBE
56. APN-154 RECEIVER ANTENNA
57. ASW-25 ANTENNA

58. RIGHT BOARDING STEPS
59. GROUND FUELING PANEL AND
    EXTERNAL POWER CONNECTOR
60. RIGHT FUSELAGE FORMATION LIGHT
61. EXTENSIBLE EQUIPMENT PLATFORM
62. CHAFF DISPENSERS
63. LOWER UHF/IFF ANTENNA
64. ARRESTING HOOK
65. RADAR ALTIMETER ANTENNAS
66. FUSELAGE FUEL DUMP OUTLET
67. ALQ-126 TRANSMITTER ANTENNAS

Features of the ICAP-2, Block 86 Prowler are identified in this general arrangement drawing. Block 89 aircraft have the same features except that the radome and antenna for the USQ-113 communications jammer are being added to the underside of the aft fuselage on some of these aircraft.

(U. S. Navy)

BuNo. 162936 was one of thirty-five ICAP-2, Block 82 Prowlers built before the introduction of Block 86 improvements. These EA-6Bs were delivered between January 1984 and June 1988. This aircraft is shown in the markings of VAQ-134, and the photograph was taken while that unit was operating from the USS KITTY HAWK, CV-63, in support of Operation Southern Watch. (Drummond)

The antenna patterns under the nose and on the spine of an ICAP-2, Block 86 Prowler can be seen in this in-flight photograph. Compare these antenna locations with those above on the Block 82 aircraft. (Drummond)

EA-6B, 163402, is one of the newest Prowlers in the Navy, and it was manufactured to Block 86 standards. It is shown here on the flight deck of the USS EISENHOWER, CVN-69, in early May 1994.

The USQ-113 radome is being installed on the aft fuselage of Block 89 aircraft as of late 1994. (Drummond)

ing Standard aircraft that were previously modified to ICAP-1s were rebuilt as ICAP-2s, as were surviving EXCAPs. Total Prowler production was 165 aircraft, not including the ETA, NEA-6Bs and five preproduction aircraft.

The most extensive upgrade to the Prowler was ADVCAP, for ADVanced CAPability. All ADVCAP aircraft were to be remanufactured Prowlers, which meant that some airframes would have flown as four of the five major variants of the Prowler. The complete ADVCAP package consisted of three parts; AIP for Avionics Improvement Program, VEP for Vehicle Enhancement Program, and a navigation systems upgrade. AIP would have replaced the entire onboard portion of the ALQ-99 with the Receiver/Processor Group (RPG). This major advance was to replace the 1960's vintage ALQ-99 receiving system with state-of-the-art electronics. A new, integrat-

*EA-6B, 156482, became the first of three aircraft to be modified in a three-step program designed to further improve the Prowler's capabilities. The aircraft was painted in an all white scheme with red, white, and blue markings. A prowling cat was painted on the nose in black, and the acronym **ADVCAP**, standing for ADVanced CAPability was lettered on the tail in black.* *(Grumman)*

ed communications jammer, the ALQ-149, was also part of the upgrade. VEP would have altered the external profile of the Prowler with the addition of an eighteen-inch "shark fin" on top of the "football" which was bulged to contain RPG components. Small strakes at the wing roots, improved efficiency flaps and slats, differential speed brakes, and new outer wing stations were other key features. The ALQ-149 also featured a large antenna attached to the "birdcage."

AIP and VEP were developed concurrently in separate aircraft. The fifth pre-production aircraft, Bureau Number 156482, which had been previously modified as the ICAP-1 prototype, became the Full Scale Development airplane for AIP. It had the RPG and ALQ-149 installed and had the bulged "football," but it had ICAP-2 cockpits. This aircraft was extensively tested by both Grumman and the Navy, and it proved the AIP concept. Bureau Number 158542 was the aerodynamic testbed for VEP, but it did not have the upgraded engines planned for ADVCAP. A third aircraft was at Grumman undergoing the full ADVCAP modification when the program was cancelled in 1993 due to budget constraints.

*The second demonstrator in the ADVCAP program was 158542. It was painted in a scheme very similar to the aircraft shown above and has the heightened vertical fin above the "football" antenna fairing. Less noticeable are the recontoured slats and flaps and the addition of wing glove strakes. The letters **VEP** on the vertical tail stand for Vehicle Enhancement Program. New J52-P409 engines and a new digital flight control system were also part of this program.* *(Grumman)*

This Prowler was one of the ICAP-1 aircraft assigned to the "Black Ravens" of VAQ-135 during the attacks against Libya in April 1986. The squadron operated from the USS CORAL SEA, CV-43, during those raids. **(Drummond)**

The Prowler in Combat

The Prowler's combat debut came not too long after its fleet introduction at NAS Whidbey Island, Washington, in 1971. VAQ-132 was the first Prowler squadron to complete training on the new aircraft and was declared operational in July 1971. VAQ-131 was the second squadron to complete training, and both units deployed to Southeast Asia in the second half of 1972. The "Scorpions" of VAQ-132 were part of Carrier Air Wing Eight in the USS AMERICA, CVA-66, while the "Lancers" of VAQ-131 were assigned to the air wing aboard the USS ENTERPRISE, CVAN-65. The "Scorpions" saw combat first when they supported strike groups from several aircraft carriers stationed off the coast of North Vietnam. VAQ-131 joined the action in September 1972. The importance of the tactical jamming provided by the Prowlers is evidenced by the "Scorpions" jumping flight decks at one point to support the USS MIDWAY, CVA-41, while the AMERICA was off station during the September time period. (The "A" has subsequently been dropped from the designations of carriers. The "A" is used here, because it was part of the carriers' designation during the time frame being discussed.)

In addition to setting the precedent of Prowler cross-decking, a fact of life for many Prowler squadrons for years to come, VAQ-132 and VAQ-131 directly supported U. S. Air Force strikes commencing with the B-52 "Arc Light" missions in November 1972. In the present era of "jointness," the coordinated and combined operations of the U. S. military services, it's interesting to note that the EA-6B was in fact a joint asset from the outset of its operational existence.

Prowlers next flew combat missions during Operation Urgent Fury in Grenada in 1983 and also supported the botched strike in Lebanon on 4 December, 1983. VAQ-137, flying from the USS JOHN F. KENNEDY, CV-67, jammed for A-6s and A-7s from the KENNEDY and the

USS INDEPENDENCE, CV-62, in the latter action. This strike was in retaliation for surface-to-air missile firings on an F-14 TARPS conducting a reconnaissance mission.

A little over two years later, on 1 January, 1986, telephones all over Whidbey Island started ringing early in the morning. CVW-13, embarked in USS CORAL SEA, CV-43, had been put on notice to strike Libya. The CORAL SEA's air wing did not include Prowlers, so the order was passed to send an EA-6B squadron to the carrier. VAQ-135 had just completed a workup period in preparation for deployment on board the AMERICA, which was scheduled to set sail on its six-month "cruise" in February 1986. Since VAQ-135 was ready to deploy, and was fresh from its recent at-sea period, the Whidbey wing tapped them, along with many augmentees from other Prowler squadrons, to join the CORAL SEA.

Just hours after being notified, ferry crews from five Prowler squadrons at Whidbey Island, flying the best seven jets from all those on the base, took off to start the trip to the Mediterranean. The aircraft stopped overnight at NAS Oceana, Virginia, and on the following day, the five top jets continued first to Spain and then on to NAS Sigonella, Sicily. Two Air Force C-141s, reportedly diverted to Whidbey in mid-flight, took VAQ-135 and the numerous additional aircrew and maintenance personnel to the east coast and then across the Atlantic.

After several months of operating off the coast of Libya, the strike against that country was finally precipitated by a terrorist bombing of a Berlin disco. Shortly after midnight local time on 15 April, aircraft launched from the CORAL SEA and the AMERICA against targets in northeastern Libya. At the same time, Air Force F-111Fs, along with EF-111As from England, were nearing their targets in Tripoli. VAQ-135 had two Prowlers airborne supporting the Navy strikes against Benina and Bengazi. VMAQ-2, at that time the only Marine Prowler squadron, sent Detachment Yankee on deployment with AMERICA

VMAQ-2 is one of two Marine Prowler squadrons, and it saw action in Operation Desert Storm. The unit is home based at Cherry Point, North Carolina, and during the Gulf War it deployed to Sheikh Isa Air Base, Bahran, with twelve EA-6Bs. One of their aircraft is shown here with an AGM-88 HARM under the right wing. Twenty-seven Prowlers were divided among the six Navy squadrons that operated from carriers during Desert Storm.
(USMC photo)

in place of VAQ-135. One "Q-2" Prowler jammed for the Navy-only strike, and Q-2 also jammed for the F-111F strike. (In addition, AMERICA's A-7s were HARM shooters for the Tripoli attack.) On the Navy attack, all of the A-6s from the two carriers returned from their successful missions. The Air Force lost one F-111F and its two crewmen with the exact cause remaining unknown.

A sometimes forgotten combat action took place in April 1988. Operation Praying Mantis was a retaliatory attack on Iranian oil platforms for the mining explosion of the frigate USS SAMUEL B. ROBERTS. In the course of the next twenty-four hours, Iranian gunboats and frigates were engaged, and several Iranian vessels were sunk. VAQ-135, this time at sea in ENTERPRISE, jammed Iranian air defense radars to negate possible Iranian air action, and they also jammed Iranian ship radars.

Six Prowler squadrons flew in Operation Desert Storm, operating from carriers in the Red Sea and the Arabian Gulf. In addition, Marine Prowlers from VMAQ-2 participated in Desert Shield and Desert Storm, flying from Shaikh Isa, Bahrain. Prowlers were literally at the forefront of the action during Desert Storm, including flying to the outskirts of Baghdad during the first large scale attack on that city shortly after the opening F-117 bomb runs. The approximately twenty-seven Navy and twelve Marine Prowlers jammed for all coalition aircraft that flew during the war. The EA-6Bs flew direct support missions over Iraq as well as flying standoff profiles from Saudi Arabia and just off the coast of Kuwait. During February 1991, Navy and Marine Prowlers in conjunction with EF-111s, provided twenty-four hour jamming coverage for the Kuwaiti Theater of Operations.

Prowler HARM capability became an important factor during the last half of Desert Storm. To preclude any "blue on blue" engagements, in other words firing weapons at our own forces, only Prowlers and F-4Gs were authorized to shoot HARMS. These two aircraft were the only HARM shooters capable of analyzing radar signals and distinguishing with certainty friend from foe.

Prowlers next saw action in January 1993, when VAQ-134 supported strike aircraft from the USS KITTY HAWK, CV-63, and the Air Force which were attacking targets in southern Iraq. Following the conclusion of Desert Storm, specific conditions were imposed upon the Iraqis, including the establishment of "no-fly" zones in northern and southern Iraq. To enforce these zones, Operation Southern Watch was implemented. Iraqi aircraft began to violate the no-fly zones, and surface-to-air missile sites were being re-established in those areas where they were not allowed. After several incidents, including Air Force shoot downs of Iraqi aircraft, the Air Force and the Navy struck on three separate days in January 1993 at various targets below the 36th parallel. VAQ-134 aircraft jammed Iraqi radars and fired HARMS in a replay of missions flown during Desert Storm.

The planning and execution of VAQ-134's Southern Watch strike missions are typical of any Prowler combat sortie. First, usually long before the carrier reaches its operating area, Prowler crews have assembled and studied the electronic order of battle (EOB). They spend time analyzing the radars and threat systems, and prioritizing targets for jamming and HARMs. Planning is done manually by plotting items on charts, looking at terrain and coordinating with the attack planners on the probable

Armed with an AGM-88, this Prowler from VAQ-134 is ready for a mission against Iraqi missiles sites during January 1993. Although the "Garudas" did not participate in Operation Desert Storm, they got in their licks during Operation Southern Watch. Note the Laser Guided Bomb under the wing of the Intruder at the far left in the photograph.
(Drummond)

strike routing. Concurrently, planning and data sorting is started on TEAMS.

For the VAQ-134 aircrews, the specific planning took place in early January after conferences with Air Force aircrews ashore at Dhahran, Saudi Arabia. The plans were refined back aboard KITTY HAWK, and the Prowler crews determined the optimum EA-6B stationing for both jamming and HARM shots. With the plans finalized, tapes were downloaded from TEAMS in preparation for the flights.

The first attack was originally scheduled for the night of 12 January, but weather precluded a strike. Prior to that night's man-up of aircraft on the flight deck, the air wing thoroughly briefed the entire event as did the separate elements (i.e., the attack aircraft, the fighters, the EW players). The weather cleared on the thirteenth, and that evening the air wing launched from KITTY HAWK, which was operating in the northern half of the Arabian Gulf.

The Southern Watch strikes were in fact coalition strikes, as aircraft from other countries also participated. VAQ-134's aircraft refueled from Royal Air Force tankers, while other aircraft from the KITTY HAWK were serviced by U. S. Air Force tankers. After checking in with AWACS, all the players proceeded across the Iraqi border to arrive on target at each particular package's scheduled time. Every aircraft in this joint mission followed a specific game plan that deconflicted aircraft over the targets at ingress and egress altitudes. My particular airplane had the westernmost target of the first night's attack. We went "jammers on" at our predetermined time as scheduled. Iraqi radar activity basically stopped as the Iraqis apparently remembered the lesson taught them during Desert Storm--where there's jamming, HARMS usually follow. No matter which choice the enemy makes, our mission of suppressing enemy radar activity is successful. Our jamming essentially blanks their scopes, and if they try to work through the jamming, a HARM is likely to hit them.

We flew our orbit, monitored the quiet radar picture, and searched for a HARM target. On our egress, a radar at an airfield turned on to track the coalition aircraft. We quickly located the target, designated a HARM package, and launched our missile. All indications are that it guided successfully. The Prowler on the easternmost package also fired a HARM. Crossing the border back into Saudi Arabian airspace, we checked out with AWACS and returned uneventfully for recovery. Although this was a relatively benign mission from our standpoint, given the lack of a creditable Iraqi air threat, a great deal of intense mission planning and threat analysis were required to successfully complete it.

This same process is still being carried out in Southern Watch over Iraq and also over Bosnia/Heregovina in late 1994. In August, Prowlers from VAQ-140 flying from the USS GEORGE WASHINGTON, CVN-73, jammed in support of United Nations forces over the former Yugoslavia. It's hard to say when or where the next major combat operation will take place, but whatever the situation, it is a safe bet to say that EA-6Bs will be there providing jamming and HARM support. Hopefully, the Prowler's good fortune will also continue. From Vietnam to the present, no EA-6B has ever been lost in combat.

The Prowler and the Raven Compared

Although dramatically different in appearance, the EA-6B and its Air Force counterpart, the EF-111A Raven, exist for the same reason--the electronic jamming of radars. As an EA-6B Electronic Counter Measures Officer, or ECMO, I've had the fortune to do an exchange tour in EF-111As. With over 1500 Prowler hours and 500 hours in the EF-111, and having flown combat missions in both, I see specific advantages and disadvantages in each of the aircraft. Because both are tactical jammers and use versions of the ALQ-99 jamming system, there are many similarities in tactics and employment. Prowlers though have several other concurrent electronic warfare roles, including electronic support (ES, to use the current phraseology), employment of the AGM-88 High speed Anti-Radiation Missile (HARM), and communications jamming. The Raven is strictly a radar jammer. but the Air Force has other aircraft that are dedicated to the ES mission, the HARM shooter role, and communications jamming.

To start off the comparison of the aircraft, a short discussion on terminology is in order. What both airplanes do, electronic jamming of radars, is known as ECM, or Electronic Countermeasures. With the recent Department of Defense change in terminology, ECM is encompassed within what is called Electronic Attack or EA. This term includes other means of waging electronic warfare such as the use of HARMs. EA better describes the Prowler's multi-mission capabilities, while ECM is the Raven's only mission. Being an impartial Prowler guy, I'll have to call this multi-mission capability an advantage for the Prowler, and I see this as being primarily due to the difference in the airframes of the two aircraft.

Differences in the airframe are responsible for the differing number of aircrew. The crew makeup of a Prowler is one pilot and three ECMOs. In a normal four person crew, each ECMO flies up front in the ECMO-1 position every third flight. As ECMO-1, we carry out the navigator duties, operate the navigation radar, handle most of the communications, and operate the communications jamming equipment. Flying in the back in ECMO-2 or -3 positions, we analyze radar signals, operate the jammers, and do the HARM targeting. This division of front seat and back seat workload allows ECMO-2 and -3 to fully concentrate on the EW mission while the front seaters concentrate on the flying of the aircraft. The sharing of the workload between four people gives the Prowler an inherent flexibility to effectively perform other tasks such as shooting HARMs and jamming communications while not detracting from the radar jamming mission.

When I first started flying in the right seat of an EF-111A, I thought I could easily accomplish the normal co-pilot duties while doing as much EW work as I did in the back seat of a Prowler. I was mistaken. The workload of the two-seat EF-111 tends to saturate the Electronic Warfare Officer, or EWO, as the right-seater is known. The crew coordination and sharing of flight duties in an EF are very good, and having just two members in a crew makes inner cockpit communication easier than in a Prowler. However, there is simply less time for the EWO to devote solely to EW. The EWO's responsibilities center on navigation, radar operation, and assigning and monitoring the jamming transmitters.

Aircraft radar systems are another difference between the two airplanes, with the advantage in this area going to the Raven. The Prowler's radar is a simplified version of the A-6 attack radar; and it is used just for navigation. The EF retains the attack radar (used for navigation), but it also has the terrain following radar (TFR) system of the F-111 bombers. The EF's ability to fly low, fast, and at night with its TFR is a very handy option when planning combat operations, and it is an ability the Prowler lacks. Even though missions during Operation Desert Storm were flown mainly at medium to high altitudes, many aircraft, including the Ravens, flew their first sorties at low level during hours of darkness. This was done to delay detection of the first wave of coalition aircraft. (After the opening strikes, the element of surprise was, shall we say, gone.)

TFR flight is very crew demanding, especially at night. The F-111's TFR, designed in the early sixties, is still a very impressive system. Unlike later infrared systems that provide a visual picture, the F-111's TFR paints the terrain in front of the aircraft and displays the ground returns next to a ride line on the TFR scope. The system guides the airplane above a Set Clearance Plane (SCP). The F-111 crews don't even look outside at night. I found it too disconcerting to look up at dark peaks on either side of my aircraft while night TFing! Doing this at 510 knots, 200 feet above the ground, at night over Iraq doesn't leave much time for signal analysis. But, even if the Prowler did have TFR capability, I doubt I'd be watching radar signals in the back seat. While flying down low, my attention would still be focused on the flight path.

The Prowler's ability to shoot HARMs is a definite advantage over the EF-111A. Instead, the Air Force relies on its F-4Gs and increasingly F-16s, and soon perhaps F-15s, to shoot HARMs. The Prowler is the second best HARM shooter in the U. S. inventory, with the F-4G Wild Weasel being the best. The F-4G's EW system, the APR-47, was designed for the sole mission of searching for and locating radars. Once the particular radar is located, the F-4G crew then proceeds to destroy the radar with HARMs or with other weapons. Prowlers however, do not do the Weasel mission. Having HARMs on a Prowler is an important additional capability that enhances the offensive capability of the EA-6B while not detracting from our primary mission of jamming.

The Raven community has several times proposed to higher authority that EF's be modified to employ HARMs, but these efforts have not been successful. The EF could easily carry up to four HARMS without any problem, since wing stores other than a cargo pod are not carried by operational Ravens.

The EA-6B has the advantage over the EF-111 when comparing each aircraft's ALQ-99 tactical jamming system. The ALQ-99F version in Prowlers today is about a generation and a half ahead of the Raven's ALQ-99E. The ALQ-99F has an upgraded computer with more power and memory and greatly expanded software in comparison to the Raven's system. The Prowler also has a greater number of jamming modes with much more sophisticated techniques. In terms of output power of the transmitters, the aircraft are roughly equal. Sorry, just how much power is classified, but trust me, it's a lot of watts.

Air Force descriptions of the ALQ-99E have for years portrayed it as the most sophisticated tactical jammer system flying operationally and have touted its fully automatic jamming capability. The ICAP-1 Prowler's ALQ-99D system had similar software and capability, but it was deleted in one of the early ALQ-99D software upgrades. Operator input to the system, what the Air Force has termed the "semi-automatic" mode, was the most effective and commonly used employment of the Prowler's system. The truth of the matter is that the Navy has, up until the cancellation of ADVCAP, continually funded hardware as well as software upgrades to the Prowler's EW system, while the Air Force has only provided software updates to the Raven fleet. (A major hardware update for the Raven, similar in scope to what was planned for ADVCAP, has been ongoing for many years, but has yet to reach the flying test and development stage.)

The Raven does have several advantages over an EA-6B that are a result of its F-111 airframe. It has greater speed capability, which allows EFs to easily keep up with any strike aircraft in either the Navy or the Air Force. It also has a greater fuel capacity, which translates to increased range or time on station. EFs normally carry a full load of ten jamming transmitters in the former bomb bay. A Prowler will usually carry three jamming pods, which results in a total of six transmitters. Two fuel tanks or one tank and a HARM are the usual combat stores for the two remaining stores stations. Carrying five jamming pods (ten transmitters) on a Prowler takes away a good deal of fuel and limits both range and time on station.

Regardless of the package, these two tactical jamming aircraft essentially do the same thing. The Navy and the Air Force tend to characterize each other's aircraft as not being quite as capable as their own. This was especially true after Desert Storm, where each service said the other's aircraft was mainly a stand-off jammer. The truth is that both aircraft flew close support as well as stand-off jamming missions. Sometimes Prowlers went deep into enemy territory, just as the EFs did on about sixty percent of their missions. Both types of aircraft spent many hours in standoff jamming orbits. Specific strike requirements drove the jamming profiles. Ravens were called upon more times to go deep and long, but it was because they could, not because their system was better.

The actual orbit patterns of the aircraft are different, due to the way the jamming transmitters are installed in the aircraft, but overall employment is the same. EA-6Bs and EF-111s will be stationed to provide the best possible electronic support based on a strike group's tactics. In a campaign such as Desert Storm, the ideal case is to have both types of aircraft. The strengths of each can then be used to best support the aircraft with the bombs. After all, that is the bottom line.

Which aircraft would I prefer to fly in combat again? Leaving aside the fact that I'm in the Navy, I'd probably have to say the Prowler. It is a more versatile platform than the Raven. But from a right seater/back seater point of view, I'll readily admit that flying in a pointy-nosed aircraft that can go supersonic on the deck without breaking a sweat is a blast. If ever someone offered me a ride in a Raven again, I certainly wouldn't turn it down!

EA-6B COCKPIT DETAILS
STANDARD & EXCAP COCKPITS

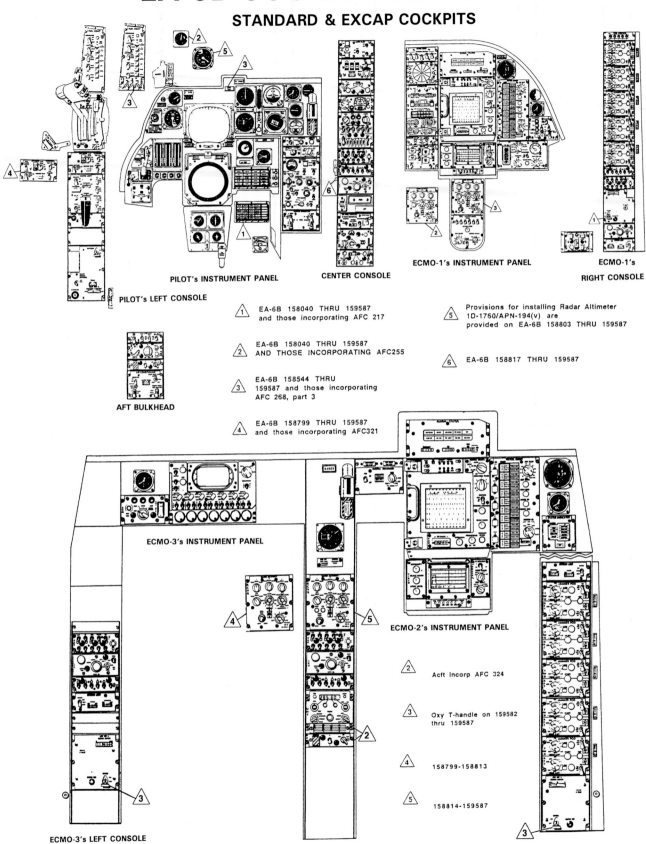

PILOT's INSTRUMENT PANEL

CENTER CONSOLE

ECMO-1's INSTRUMENT PANEL

ECMO-1's RIGHT CONSOLE

PILOT's LEFT CONSOLE

AFT BULKHEAD

⚠1 EA-6B 158040 THRU 159587 and those incorporating AFC 217

⚠2 EA-6B 158040 THRU 159587 AND THOSE INCORPORATING AFC255

⚠3 EA-6B 158544 THRU 159587 and those incorporating AFC 268, part 3

⚠4 EA-6B 158799 THRU 159587 and those incorporating AFC321

⚠5 Provisions for installing Radar Altimeter 1D-1760/APN-194(v) are provided on EA-6B 158803 THRU 159587

⚠6 EA-6B 158817 THRU 159587

ECMO-3's INSTRUMENT PANEL

ECMO-2's INSTRUMENT PANEL

ECMO-3's LEFT CONSOLE

CENTER CONSOLE

ECMO-2's RIGHT CONSOLE

⚠2 Acft Incorp AFC 324

⚠3 Oxy T-handle on 159582 thru 159587

⚠4 158799-158813

⚠5 158814-159587

On this and the next three pages are drawings of the different cockpit layouts used in various EA-6B upgrades. In each case, cockpit colors would be similar to those shown on pages 36 through 39 for an ICAP-2, Block 86 aircraft. The cockpit layout as found in EXCAP Prowlers is shown in these drawings. It differed very little from the layout in Standard EA-6Bs.

(U. S. Navy)

ICAP-1 COCKPITS

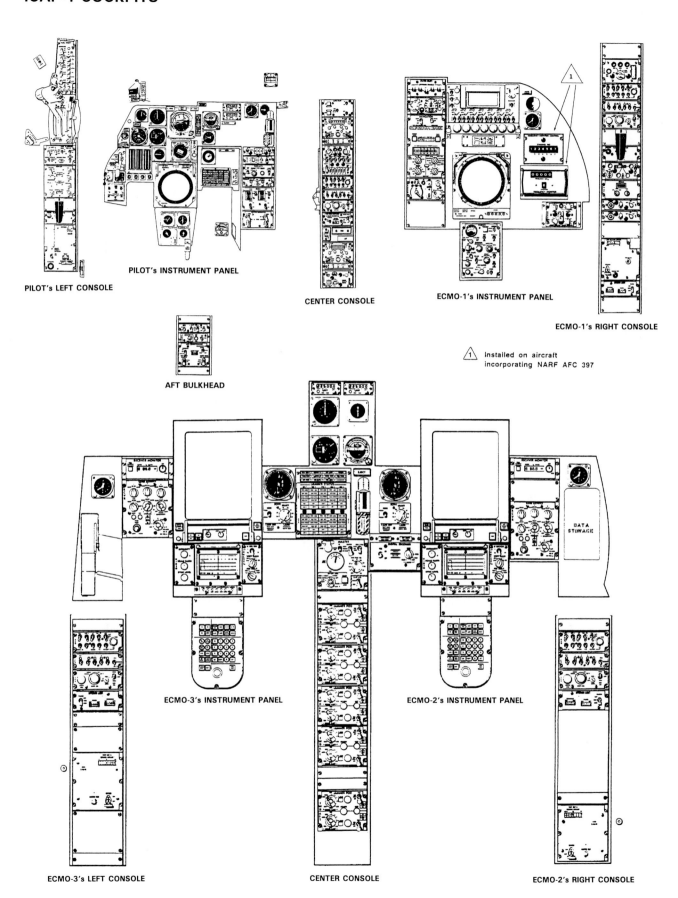

PILOT's LEFT CONSOLE

PILOT's INSTRUMENT PANEL

CENTER CONSOLE

ECMO-1's INSTRUMENT PANEL

ECMO-1's RIGHT CONSOLE

AFT BULKHEAD

⚠1 Installed on aircraft
incorporating NARF AFC 397

DATA STORAGE

ECMO-3's INSTRUMENT PANEL

ECMO-2's INSTRUMENT PANEL

ECMO-3's LEFT CONSOLE

CENTER CONSOLE

ECMO-2's RIGHT CONSOLE

The drawings on this page show the cockpits as found in ICAP-1 Prowlers.

(U. S. Navy)

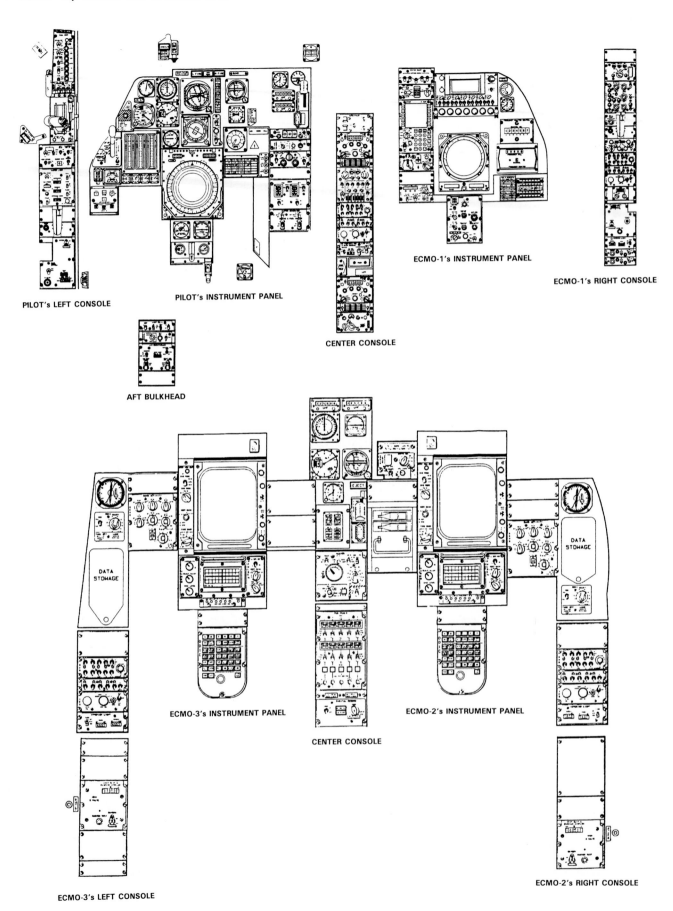

PILOT's LEFT CONSOLE

PILOT's INSTRUMENT PANEL

AFT BULKHEAD

CENTER CONSOLE

ECMO-1's INSTRUMENT PANEL

ECMO-1's RIGHT CONSOLE

ECMO-3's INSTRUMENT PANEL

ECMO-2's INSTRUMENT PANEL

CENTER CONSOLE

ECMO-3's LEFT CONSOLE

ECMO-2's RIGHT CONSOLE

The layout of the original cockpits in ICAP-2, Block 82 aircraft looked like this.

(U. S. Navy)

ICAP-2, BLOCK 86 & BLOCK 89 COCKPITS

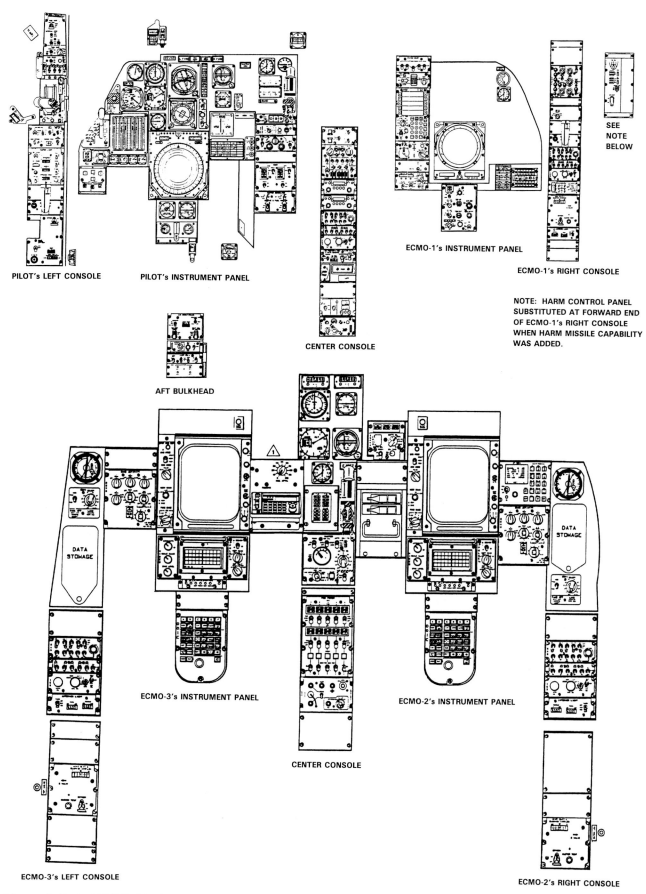

PILOT's LEFT CONSOLE

PILOT's INSTRUMENT PANEL

ECMO-1's INSTRUMENT PANEL

ECMO-1's RIGHT CONSOLE

SEE
NOTE
BELOW

NOTE: HARM CONTROL PANEL
SUBSTITUTED AT FORWARD END
OF ECMO-1's RIGHT CONSOLE
WHEN HARM MISSILE CAPABILITY
WAS ADDED.

CENTER CONSOLE

AFT BULKHEAD

DATA STOWAGE

DATA STOWAGE

ECMO-3's INSTRUMENT PANEL

ECMO-2's INSTRUMENT PANEL

CENTER CONSOLE

ECMO-3's LEFT CONSOLE

ECMO-2's RIGHT CONSOLE

The cockpits in ICAP-2, Block 86 Prowlers are shown in these drawings. Block 89 aircraft differed only very slightly from what is shown here.

(U. S. Navy)

17

PROWLER DETAILS

ECM PODS

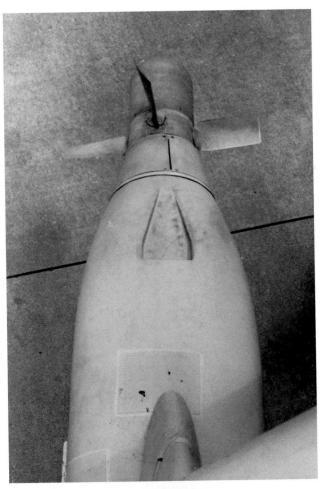

Above: The Prowler's main "armament" has always been its ALQ-99 electronic countermeasures pods. Over the years, considerable changes have been made to the electronic equipment carried in these pods, but their external appearance has not changed very much. At first glance, the ALQ-99 may appear to be the same as the ALQ-76 pod used on the EA-6A (see page 57), but there are a number of differences. ALQ-76 pods have flat sides and four panels along each side. The ALQ-99 has a contoured side and only three panels. The front and rear panels are unpainted radiators to cool the exciters carried inside the pod. In this photograph, the wedge-shaped spacer between the pod and the wing pylon can be seen. This spacer is used between ECM pods and the wing pylons, but none is used between a pod and the centerline station. Also note that this spacer is not present when a fuel tank is carried as seen on the inboard pylon.

Above right: This top view of the forward end of an ALQ-99 ECM pod shows the vanes for the ram air turbine or RAT. Also visible is the shape of the inlet slot just aft of the RAT. The RAT provides electrical power for the pod.

The Prowler can carry two types of ALQ-99 pods. These two photographs show a high band pod from the front and the rear. Note the cross section of the pod and that the sides are almost flat. This is the same pod as shown in the top left photograph.

A common misconception about the ALQ-99 ECM pods is that high band pods are only carried on the wing pylons, and low band pods are carried on the centerline station. This is incorrect. Both types of pods can be carried on any of the five stations in any combination. This is a front view of a high band pod on the centerline pylon.

From the side, the ALQ-99 low band pod looks to have essentially the same appearance as the high band pod. This photograph shows a low band pod attached to a Prowler's left outboard wing pylon which is station 1. Note that the wedge-shaped spacer is again present with the low band pod.
(Detail & Scale collection)

When viewed from the front or the rear, the low band pod reveals its much wider base or keel. Compare the cross section shown in this rear view with that of the high band pod illustrated on the previous page.
(Detail & Scale collection)

EJECTION SEATS

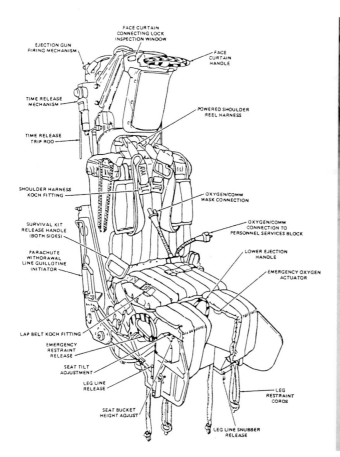

The ejection seat used in the EA-6B is the Martin Baker GRUEA-7. Firing of the seats is timed to eject all four members of the crew in sequence to provide safe separation. At left is a drawing of the seat with its various features indicated by callouts. At right is a right front view of a seat that is ready for installation in the aircraft.

(Left U. S. Navy, right Detail & Scale collection)

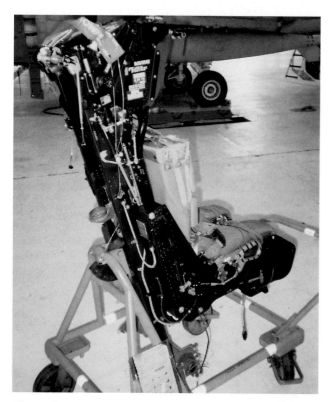

These two photographs show additional details of the GRUEA-7 ejection seat. *(Both Detail & Scale collection)*

WINDSCREEN & CANOPIES

This overall view from above shows the windscreen and canopies to good effect. Although it is difficult to see in a photograph, the two canopies have a slight gold tint, while the windscreen does not. Note that the forward canopy is larger than the rear one.

Just forward of the pilot's windscreen glass is a set of vents for the rain removal system. The fairing just forward of the vent is for a red light that illuminates the refueling probe during night refuelings.

(Detail & Scale collection)

A light system is located on the inside of the center framing of each canopy.

At left is a side view of the right hinge for the forward canopy. At right is a look at both hinges for the rear canopy as seen from behind. Note that each hinge has a small door or panel at its aft end.

Details of the nose landing gear can be seen in this view from the left side.

This close-up provides a better look at the details of one of the nose wheels.

The forward nose gear door is shown here. Note the taxi light and the three landing attitude indicator lights.

Details of the right side of the nose gear are visible in this photograph. Also note the three tie down chains.

Electrical wiring to the taxi light and the landing attitude indicator lights can be seen on the inside of the forward main landing gear door. The insides of the doors and wells are painted gloss white, and the doors are outlined in red.

The doors on either side of the nose gear well can be seen here. Note that the left door has a series of vents on it, and these fit into a slot in the right door.

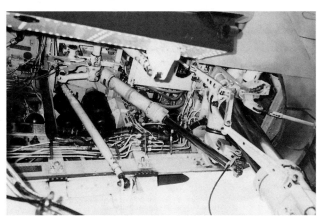

The forward portion of the nose landing gear well is visible in this view.

At left is a view looking up, aft, and to the left in the nose gear well. The photograph at right looks up, aft, and slightly to the right.

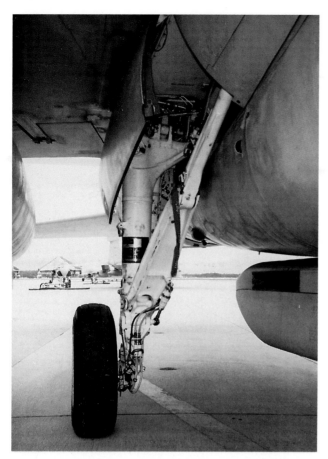 

The right main landing gear is shown from the front in the left photograph, while at right is a view from directly behind the gear.

Details of the brakes, hydraulic lines, and oleo can be seen in these two pictures of the inside of the right gear wheel.

When the aircraft is on the ground, the forward main gear doors are usually left open as seen at left. However, on some occasions, they are left closed as shown in the photo at right.

This is the forward end of the right main gear well where the retraction strut attaches to the airframe.

The aft end of the right main gear well is shown here, and the large hinge for the gear strut is clearly visible.

The inside of the aft right main gear door can be seen in this view.

LEFT MAIN LANDING GEAR

The forward main gear doors on the Prowler are different than those on an Intruder. This is because the wing fairings in front of the doors are smaller and of a different shape than those on the Intruder. At left is a photograph of the left forward main gear doors on an Intruder, while at right is a view of the same area on a Prowler. Note the different fairing on the wing and how it carries over onto the door. *(Both Detail & Scale collection)*

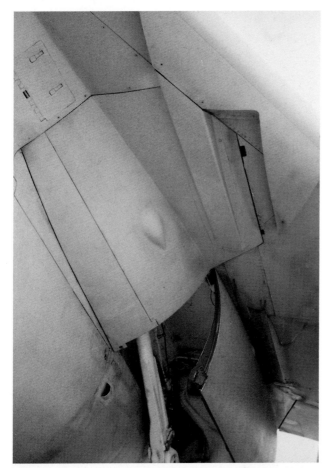

The left main landing gear wheel is seen from the outside in the photograph above, and from the inside in the one below.

The same doors are shown here again from below, but this time the doors are closed. This photograph further illustrates the different fairing found on the Prowler and how it continues on to the forward main gear doors. The doors on the right side are a mirror image of what is shown here. *(Detail & Scale collection)*

Details of the forward end of the left main gear well are visible here.

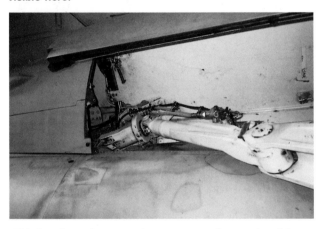

This is where the retracting strut attaches to the airframe near the forward end of the well.

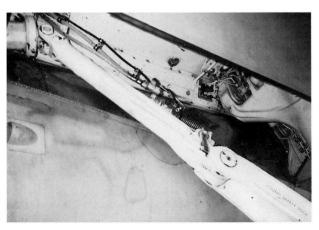

Although it is a little difficult to see in this photograph, the inner wall of the gear well (directly above the engine) is natural metal, while the rest of the well is gloss white.

Note the close proximity of the aft door to the main strut in this view taken from directly behind the left landing gear.

The aft end of the left main gear well and the strut hinge are visible here.

The distinctive cross section of the radome is shown here as are the offset refueling probe and the pitot tubes on each side of the fuselage. Note the small red light forward of the pilot's windscreen. This is used for illuminating the refueling probe during night aerial refuelings.

(Detail & Scale collection)

On EA-6Bs, up to and including the original ICAP-2, Block 82 version, there was a large blade antenna for the ALQ-92 system under the nose. Forward of it was the smaller black IFF blade antenna. This is to the left in the photo.

The underside of the nose of Block 86 and Block 89 aircraft looks like this. Just forward of the lower anti-collision light is the APN-154 radar beacon transmit antenna. The black blade antenna aft of the light is the forward TACAN antenna, while the larger swept blade is the V/UHF Number 2 lower antenna.

On each side of the forward fuselage, there is a step that folds down just below the forward cockpit. This is to provide a place for the pilot and ECMO-1 to step from the top of the engine inlet into the forward cockpit. At left is the open step on the right side of the aircraft, and at right is a view looking down at the step on the left side. The inside of the step and its well are painted gloss insignia red, and there is often a black non-skid area.

FUSELAGE TOP

The photographs on this page show the spine of the fuselage on a Block 86 Prowler. Just aft of the rear canopy is the upper anti-collision light. The antenna just aft of the light is the V/UHF Number 1 upper antenna.

The oval-shaped fairing on the spine is the upper UHF/ADF antenna.

Forward is to the left in this view. From left to right are the upper anti-collision light, the V/UHF Number 1 upper antenna, the upper UHF/IFF antenna, the UHF/ADF antenna, and the V/UHF Number 2 upper antenna. Note also the two small vents on the side of the fuselage.

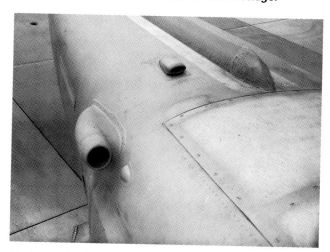

Up through the original ICAP-2, Block 82 variant of the Prowler, there was a large scoop on each side of the fuselage. The one on the right side, which is shown here, is for the air conditioning system. The one on the left side was for the ALQ-92 system. When this system was deleted from the aircraft, the scoop was replaced with a plate to cover the hole in the side of the aircraft. The smaller scoop in this photograph is the fuel vent scoop.

The long fairing leading forward from the vertical tail houses the HF antenna. Note that this fairing has a constant triangular cross section. Non-skid walkways are sometimes light gray, dark gray, or a combination of both as seen on this Prowler.

FUSELAGE UNDERSIDES

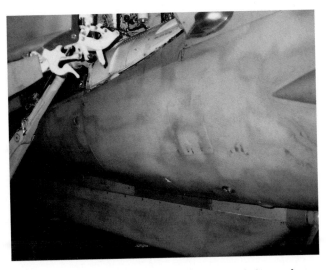

An important difference between the Intruder and the Prowler is that the Intruder has armor plate around the engines, while the Prowler does not. The photograph at left is of an Intruder's right engine, and the armor plate is visible just aft of the two black lines. At right is a similar view of a Prowler, and it is evident that there is no armor. Armor was also under the Intruder's wings and under the tail section, as illustrated elsewhere in this book.

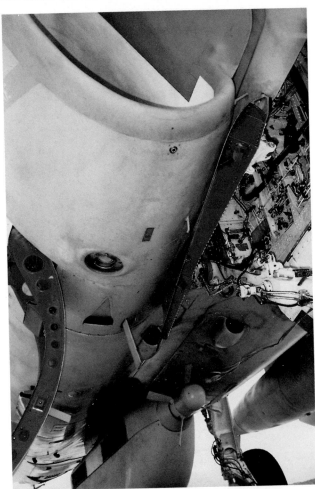

This photograph provides a different view of the area shown at left, however, it is of a different aircraft. The shape of the ASW-25 blade antenna is easier to see here. The single-point refueling receptacle is natural metal. Also notice the small slot in the right nose gear door. This is the slot that the vents shown on page 23 fit into when the doors are closed.   (Detail & Scale collection)

The underside of the right inlet is shown here. The large circular item is the single-point refueling receptacle. Just aft of it is a NACA scoop. The ASW-25 blade antenna is just inboard of this scoop. Two engine bay cooling scoops can be seen near the centerline of the aircraft and just a little further aft. There is also a small drain next to the right nose gear door.

The underside of the lower center fuselage is shown here from the front left. The small black blade antenna is for the IFF system. As seen in the top right photograph on page 20, the IFF blade antenna was located under the nose on EA-6Bs up through ICAP-2, Block 82 aircraft, but it was moved to this location under the left inlet on Block 86 Prowlers. The forward TACAN antenna replaced the IFF antenna under the nose.

 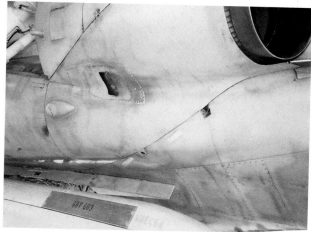

These two views show the lower fuselage around the aft end of the centerline station. Note the panel line between the lower engine exhaust cover and the fuselage. Along each panel line are two hook-shaped oil drains which face parallel to the panel line rather than to the centerline of the aircraft. Aft engine bay cooling scoops and vents are also visible in these pictures.

(Both Detail & Scale collection)

 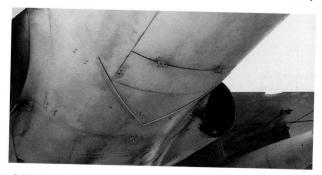

The centerline station is shown here from the left rear.

A V-shaped oil deflector is located on the underside of the fuselage just forward of the extensible equipment platform or "birdcage." This device was designed to deflect oil away from the "birdcage" and the former AN/APN-153(V) Doppler antenna fairing that was located on the door of the platform on Intruders up through the ICAP-2, Block 82 upgrade.

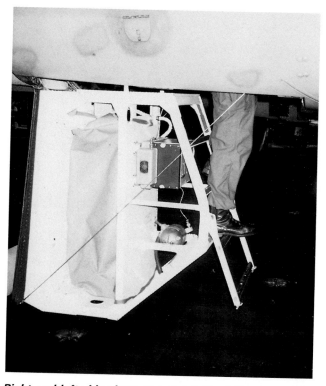 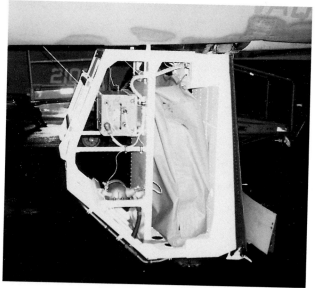

Right and left side views reveal details of the extensible equipment platform in the open position. There is a folding ladder on the forward end of the birdcage (when it is in the lowered position) that assists in gaining access to the interior of the aft fuselage. A crewman is making use of this ladder in the photo at left.

AFT FUSELAGE

The exhaust for the air conditioning system is located aft of the engine exhaust on the right side of the fuselage. It is usually bare metal as shown here, but in some cases it is painted the same color as the aircraft.

Although not originally installed on Prowlers, formation strip lights were later added to the sides of the fuselage. Unlike most other aircraft, these light panels were not fitted to the EA-6B's nose or tail sections. The circular item between the **N** and the **A** is the pressure gage for the tail hook.

There are two chaff/flare dispensers located under the aft fuselage in between the forward area of the tail hook yoke.

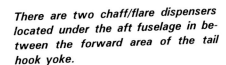

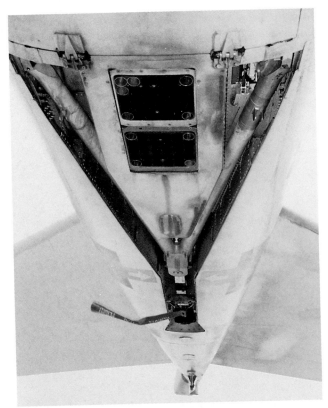

The tail hook is Y-shaped, and it can be seen from the forward end in the photograph at left. At right is the aft end of the hook. Originally the entire hook was striped, but now only the base of the Y is striped. Stripes are often two shades of gray, but in this case black and white stripes have been applied.

EA-6A COLORS

This EA-6A is from VMCJ-1, Detachment-101 based at MCAS Iwakuni, Japan. The aircraft is painted in the original light gull gray over white paint scheme and carries colorful markings. This photograph was taken on 3 April, 1975.   (Flightleader collection)

Also in the gray over white scheme, EA-6A, 156988, is painted in the markings of VAQ-33's "Firebirds." This squadron was part of the Fleet Electronic Warfare Support Group and was used for EW training. An ALE-41 chaff dispenser is attached to the outboard left wing pylon while an ALQ-76 ECM pod is carried on the inboard pylon. This photograph was taken in September 1985.
(Flightleader)

By the time this photograph was taken in December 1982, the Navy and Marines had begun changing over to tactical paint schemes for their combat aircraft. EA-6A, 151597, was assigned to Marine squadron VMAQ-4. This unit was known as the "Seahawks" and was based at NAS Whidbey Island, Washington. It now operates EA-6Bs.
(Grove via Flightleader)

Also painted in the tactical scheme, EA-6A, 156987, comes to a stop after catching a wire aboard the USS LEXINGTON, AVT-16, in May 1987. The aircraft was assigned to VAQ-209, which was part of Reserve Carrier Air Wing Twenty (CVWR-20). No Intruder variants operated routinely from ESSEX class carriers, however carrier qualifications for A-6, EA-6A, and KA-6Ds were sometimes flown aboard LEXINGTON. The famous carrier is now a museum in Corpus Christi, Texas.

EA-6B PAINT SCHEMES
COLORFUL PAINT SCHEMES

VAQ-135 is known as the "Black Ravens," and their early colorful markings included a black raven motif on the tail of the aircraft. Blue and green stripes ran almost the entire length of the fuselage. (Huston via Flightleader)

Test and evaluation units also fly Prowlers, and before the introduction of tactical paint schemes, these were among the most colorful EA-6Bs assigned to any unit. BuNo. 156478 was assigned to the Naval Air Test Center when this photograph was taken in March 1977.

(Zink via Flightleader)

VMAQ-2 is one of only two Marine squadrons ever to become operational in the EA-6B, and it is based at Cherry Point, North Carolina. For many years, the unit's markings were quite well known and included the bunny logo of "Playboy" magazine as seen in this photograph taken in April 1982. The squadron's nickname also was the "Playboys." Recently however, the unit was forced to change its name to "Panthers" in order to be "politically correct." "Panthers" was chosen because it is the name of the National Football League's new team in Charlotte, North Carolina.

(Grove via Flightleader)

TACTICAL PAINT SCHEMES

Taken on the same day as the bottom photograph on the previous page, this picture shows the changeover to tactical paint schemes in the early 1980s. Again, the aircraft is from VMAQ-2, but all color is gone leaving only gray on gray markings. Note that this aircraft has the lighter undersides originally specified for the tactical scheme used on Prowlers. This lighter color was Federal Standard 36495, the middle shade of gray was 36320, and the darker color was 35237.
(Grove via Flightleader)

The light 36495 was soon replaced with 36375, which was closer in shade to the 36320. This remains standard today. The three shades of gray are very difficult to discern except when the aircraft has been recently painted. These grays can be seen on this EA-6B from VAQ-136. All three are particularly easy to see on the nose. (Grove via Flightleader)

After even minimal weathering and spot painting, the three shades of gray become harder to distinguish as seen on this Prowler from VAQ-138. Note the yellow jacket motif on the rudder. It may enhance combat survivability to paint aircraft in the tactical scheme, but compare the way this aircraft looks to the colorful EA-6B from the same squadron that is pictured on the front cover of this book. It should also be noted that the darker shade of gray is sometimes not used.
(Grove via Flightleader)

EA-6B COCKPIT DETAILS & COLORS
FRONT COCKPIT

The photographs on this page and the next three provide an in-depth look at the colors and details inside the cockpit of an EA-6B Prowler. These photos were all taken in Block 86 aircraft, but the colors would apply to all variants. Detail differences between the various versions of Prowler can be determined by checking the drawings on pages 15 through 18. At left is the pilot's station showing the control column, flight instruments and gages, and the radar scope. At right is the coaming just above the instrument panel. It is nothing more than a flexible cover.

Details of the left console in the forward cockpit can be seen here. The main feature is the throttle quadrant with the two throttles.

This view looks almost straight down at the pilot's seat and the control column. The right two gages on the panel directly below the radar display indicator can be seen here.

The two left gages below the radar display indicator and the left rudder pedal are visible in this photo.

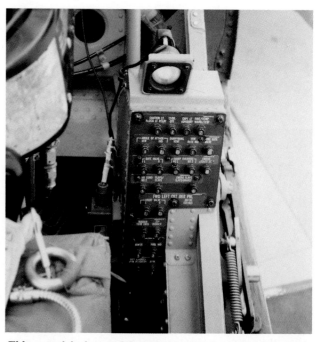

This panel is located just behind and to the left of the pilot's seat.   (Detail & Scale collection)

This is the ECMO-1's side of the forward instrument panel. The open hole at the top is where the ALQ-149 panel would have gone had the system not been cancelled.

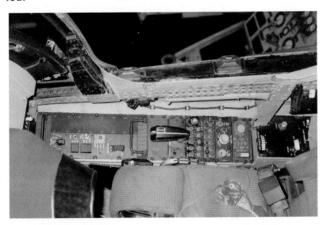

Details of the ECMO-1's right side console are illustrated in this view.

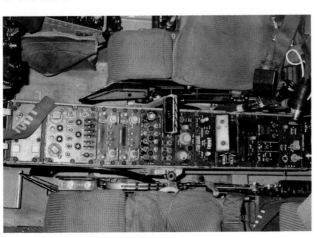

The radar control panel just below the scope can be seen here. *(Detail & Scale collection)*

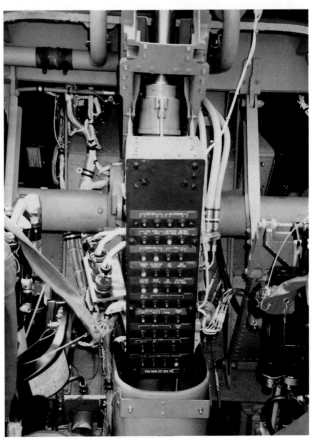

At left is a photograph looking straight down at the center console that is located between the pilot and ECMO-1. At right is the panel which is located between the two forward ejection seats and just below the mechanism that raises and lowers the front canopy.

REAR COCKPIT

In the present division of crew responsibilities, ECMO-2 and ECMO-3 perform basically the same tasks in the rear cockpit. ECMO-2 sits in the right seat behind ECMO-1, while the left seat behind the pilot is occupied by ECMO-3. This photograph shows the top portion of the main instrument panel in the rear cockpit.

This is the instrument panel at the ECMO-3's postion.

The major displays and panels at the ECMO-2's position are visible here.

Removal of the rear canopy for maintenance permitted an opportunity to take this head-on photo of most of the rear instrument panel. It provides a look at the features and details from a different angle. Note the object that appears to be a small white dot where the ECMO-3's right foot would go. This is a mike switch for the intercom system. This feature is found at each of the ECMO positions. The left foot operates a similar switch for the aircraft's radios.   (Detail & Scale collection)

Digital display indicator control panels are located between each of the ECMO's knees in the rear cockpit. The tactical jamming pod power control panel is at the center of the cockpit between the two crewmen.

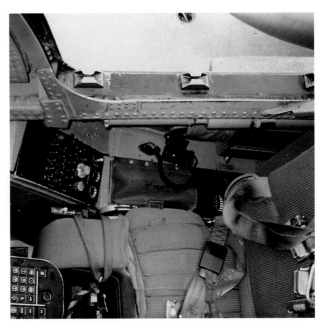

At left is the left console in the rear cockpit, while at right is the right console. Switches for the intercom system and controls for oxygen and the "G" suit connection are found on these consoles.

The entire center console is revealed at left, while at right is the mechanism for raising and lowering the rear canopy. Note that there is no panel here as there was in the forward cockpit.

RADAR & ELECTRONICS BAYS

With the radome removed from the aircraft, details of the APS-130 radar can be seen here. This is a simplified version of the radar found in the attack variants of the Intruder, and it is used for navigation purposes in the Prowler.   (Detail & Scale collection)

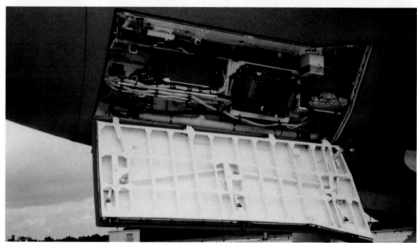

There is an equipment bay on each side of the Prowler's nose section, and this is the bay on the left side. The forward box, to the left in the photograph, is the HF radio encryption gear, while the larger box aft of it is the transceiver for the APS-130 radar.

In the right bay are several more pieces of equipment. On the top shelf at the forward end of the bay are the inertial navigation unit (forward) and a box for the ASW-25 automatic carrier landing system (aft). On the lower shelf at the forward end is the reference signal generator for the APS-130 radar. In the center section of the bay are small boxes associated with the ARC-182 U/VHF radio equipment, and at the aft end is the spherical container for the pressurized air that raises the canopies.

1/72nd SCALE FIVE-VIEW DRAWINGS

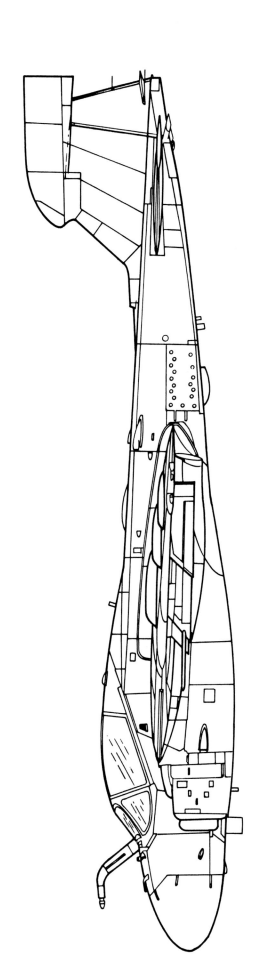

EA-6A ELECTRIC INTRUDER, LEFT SIDE VIEW

NOTE: ALL EA-6B DRAWINGS ARE OF AN ICAP-2, BLOCK 86 PROWLER

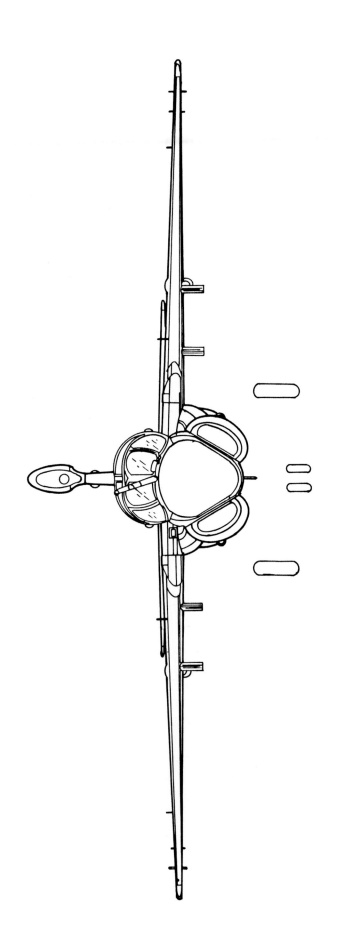

EA-6B, FRONT VIEW

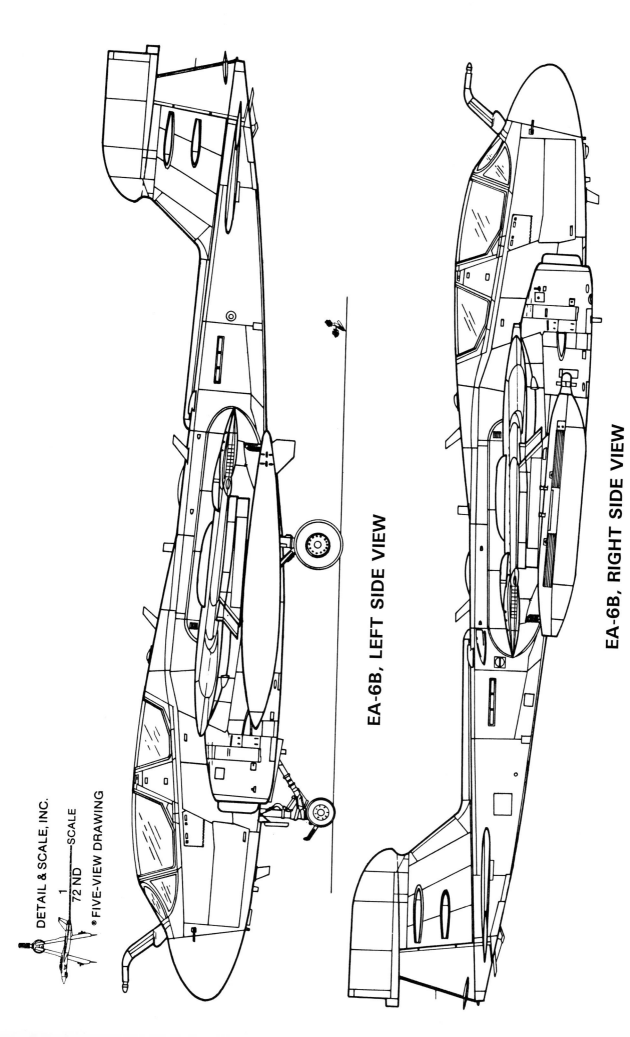

EA-6B, LEFT SIDE VIEW

EA-6B, RIGHT SIDE VIEW

DETAIL & SCALE, INC.

1
72 ND —— SCALE

® FIVE-VIEW DRAWING

DETAIL & SCALE COPYRIGHT DRAWING BY DANA BELL

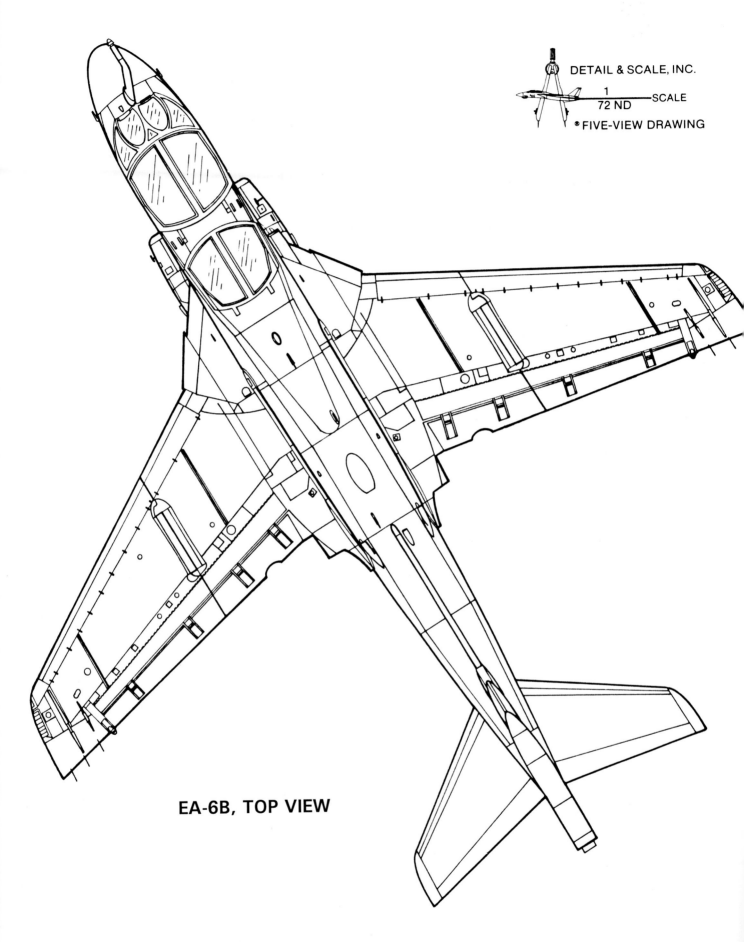

DETAIL & SCALE, INC.

$\dfrac{1}{72\text{ ND}}$ SCALE

® FIVE-VIEW DRAWING

EA-6B, TOP VIEW

DETAIL & SCALE COPYRIGHT DRAWING BY DANA BELL

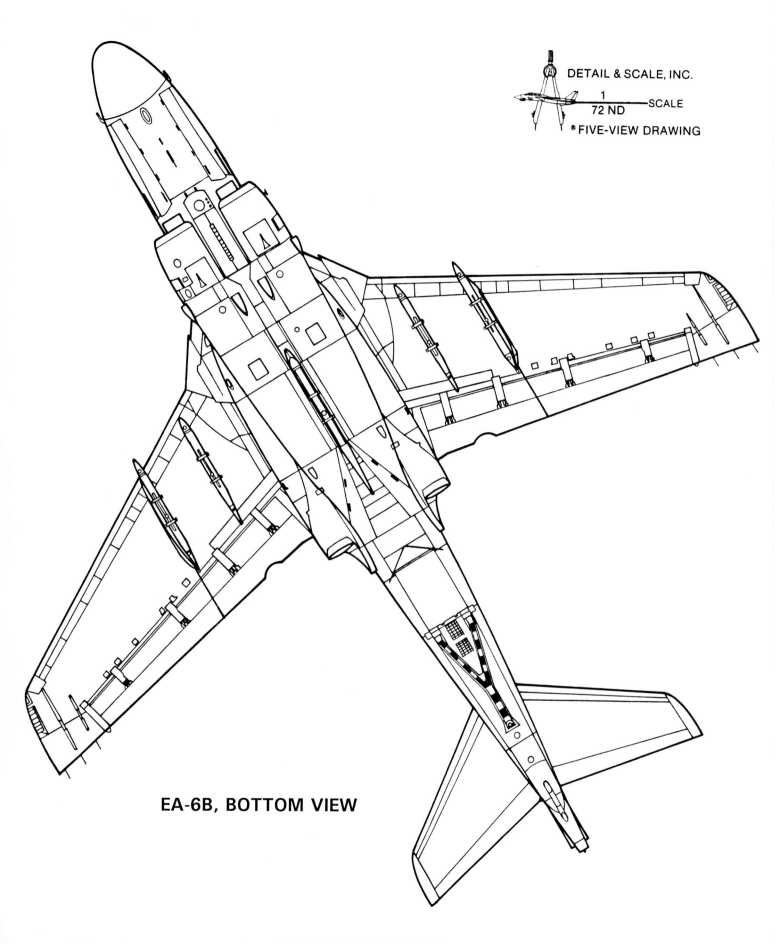

DETAIL & SCALE, INC.

$$\frac{1}{72\ ND}$$ SCALE

® FIVE-VIEW DRAWING

EA-6B, BOTTOM VIEW

DETAIL & SCALE COPYRIGHT DRAWING BY DANA BELL

INLET & ENGINE DETAILS

The engine inlets are seen from above in these two photographs. Note that there is a small flat area on top of the forward part of each inlet with some non-skid material on it. This forms a small step for the pilot and ECMO-1 to use when stepping forward to the front cockpit. On the left intake, the total temperature probe can be seen, and on the right intake is the angle-of-attack probe.

The left inlet is shown above with the boarding steps closed. Note the total temperature probe within the JET INTAKE WARNING marking. The photograph below is a close-up of the total temperature probe on another aircraft. It can also be seen from above in the top left photo on this page.

(Above author, below Detail & Scale collection)

This side view of the right inlet shows the boarding steps in the lowered position. This is the same arrangement as found on standard Intruders, except that the end of the steps are slightly different in order to conform with the different shape of the top of the Prowler's inlets when closed. Note that when the steps are open, a small cover springs forward over the angle of attack probe to protect it from being stepped on.

The interior of the right inlet is revealed in this photograph. Note that it is painted flat white. The forward end of the engine is natural metal and is seven feet from the forward end of the inlet. (Detail & Scale collection)

An entire engine, complete with its exhaust pipe, has been removed from an aircraft and placed on a service cart. This provides a better look at the engine's details. (Drummond)

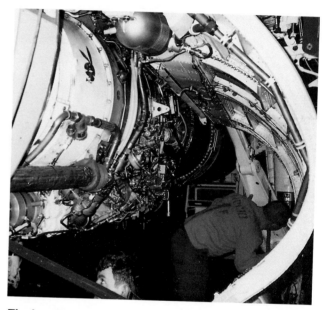

The installed left engine can be seen in this photograph.

This is the right engine bay with the J52-P-408 engine installed. Note the connection for ground electrical power in the right front of the photograph.

This photograph was taken near the aft end of the right engine and looks forward.

The exhaust fairing for the right engine is shown here.

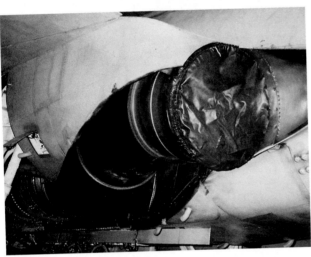

With the lower covers removed, the exhaust pipes are revealed in these two photographs. Note that these pipes are not straight but are slightly S-shaped instead.

At left is a look into the left exhaust pipe showing the aft end of the engine in the background. At right is a similar view inside of the right exhaust pipe.

WING DETAILS

Prowlers have full span leading edge slats that are usually closed when the aircraft is on the ground. Careful examination of this photograph will reveal two small probes near the tip of the slat's leading edge. These probes are designed to catch the netting of the barricade whenever an emergency recovery is required aboard a carrier.

Trailing edge flaps cover almost the full span of the wings. Just forward of the flaps are the flaperons which provide roll control for the aircraft. There are no ailerons on the Prowler.

The leading edge slats are shown here in the extended position. The area under the slats is painted gloss insignia red. Also note the shapes and locations of the two wing fences.　*(Detail & Scale collection)*

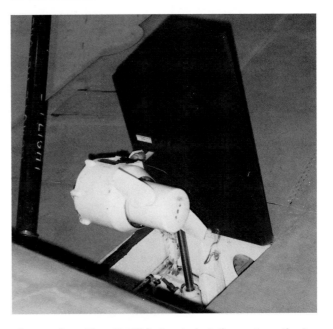

A ram air turbine (RAT) is located at the root on the top of the left wing. The RAT provides emergency electrical power to the aircraft through the use of a generator which is driven by the airflow passing over the wing.
(Detail & Scale collection)

WING BOTTOM

 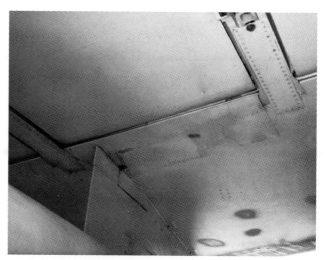

Intruders have armor plating under the wings just forward of the trailing edge flaps as seen in the photograph at left. This photograph was chosen because part of the armor had just been painted, and the fresh paint helps illustrate where the armor is located. But also note that there is another armor plate inboard (to the left in the photograph) of the pylon. It should be noted that this photograph shows the trailing edge of the inboard pylon under the right wing. The same armor is present under the left wing. The photograph at right is of the same area under the right wing of a Prowler. Note that the armor is not present on the EA-6B.

The underside of the right wing is shown here. Note the hinges for the leading edge flaps.

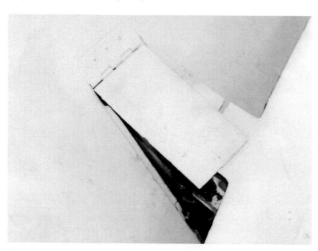

This close-up shows the details of one of the flap hinges.

The underside of the left wing flap is visible here.

WING FOLD DETAILS

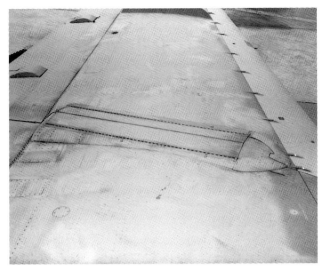 

The original wing fold hinge as used on Intruders was changed when the composite wings were fitted, so Intruders had two different designs at the wing fold. However, the wing fold hinge used on Prowlers was different from either of the two used on Intruders. On the top of each wing was a fairing with two hinged covers. The actual wing fold hinge was inside the fairing beneath the panels. At left is the fairing on top of the left wing, while at right is the fairing on the right wing.

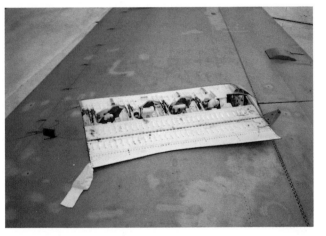 

In this view, the panels have been opened to show the hinge mechanism beneath them.

(Detail & Scale collection)

This is what the top wing fold fairing looks like when the wing is folded. (Detail & Scale collection)

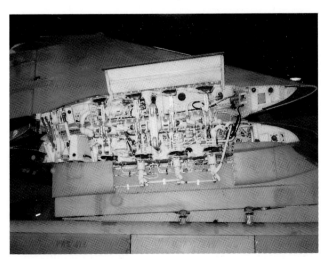 

Details of the wing fold hinges are shown from the outside in these two photographs. Note the fairing on the outboard pylon which is also part of the folding mechanism.

WING TIP DETAILS

The top of the left wing tip can be seen here. Visible are the upper hinges for the speed brake, the static dischargers, and the fuel dump fairing just inboard of the speed brake.

The fairings for the wing tip speed brakes are quite large as illustrated in this view.

There is a navigation light at the forward corner of each wing tip, and a position light panel is located at the center of each tip.

The inside of the speed brakes are painted gloss insignia red.   (Detail & Scale collection)

Just inboard of each speed brake is a fuel dump vent with a fairing above it. At left is a close-up of the vent and fairing on the left wing. This is quite different from the design used on the composite wing of the A-6E Intruder which is shown as a comparison in the photograph at right.

WING PYLONS

This is the left outboard wing pylon showing the fairing for part of the wing fold mechanism and the wedge-shaped spacer used between the pylon and the ECM pod.

The left inboard wing pylon is shown here from the front and slightly inboard. Note that there is no spacer between the pylon and the fuel tank.

This is the right outboard wing pylon.

The right inboard pylon can be seen here with a fuel tank attached.

The only armament certified for use on the Prowler is the AGM-88 HARM anti-radiation missile. HARMs can be carried on any wing pylon. A LAU-118 launcher is attached to the pylon, and the missile is carried on it rather than directly on the pylon. This is a live missile loaded on an EA-6B during Operation Southern Watch.

(Drummond)

At the top of the trailing edge of each outboard pylon is a small light. On Intruders, both of these lights are amber, but on Prowlers the light on the left inboard pylon is red and the one of the right inboard pylon (shown here) is green. These lights reflect off the lowered flaps as the aircraft approaches a carrier for a night landing, and the colors provide an identification feature for the LSO so that he can determine if the aircraft is an Intruder or a Prowler.

TAIL DETAILS

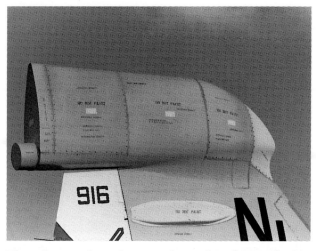

The tail cap radome is more often referred to as the "football," and inside of it are antennas for bands 4 through 9. Beginning with ICAP-1 aircraft, an ALQ-126 receiver antenna was added to the aft end. This is usually called the "beer can." On each side of the vertical tail are two fairings. The top one is the band I antenna, and the lower one is the band II antenna.

The photo above shows a section of armor plating just forward of the fuselage fuel dump on an Intruder. Below is a photograph of the fuel dump on a Prowler from a different angle. Note that the EA-6B does not have the armor plating.

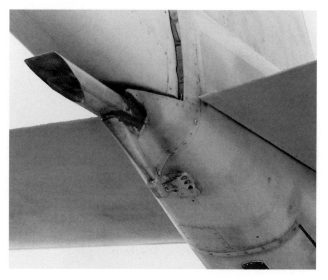

The rudder is shown here from the right side. Note that the fairing at the bottom actually moves with the rudder rather than being a part of the aft fuselage.

The fairing at the base of the rudder originally contained the ALQ-41 and ALQ-100 receiver antennas. Beginning with ICAP-1 aircraft, it was fitted with the ALQ-126 transmitter antennas.

The right horizontal stabilizer can be seen above, and the left stabilizer is shown below. The EA-6B has an all-flying tail, meaning that the entire surface of the horizontal stabilizers move to provide pitch control for the aircraft. Note that there is a rough non-skid walkway at the root of each stabilizer.

The entire tail section can be seen in this photograph taken from the superstructure of the USS EISENHOWER.

EA-6A ELECTRIC INTRUDER

Carrying AN/ALQ-53 ECM reconnaissance pods on its outboard pylons, one of the early EA-6As (originally designated A2F-1H) is shown during an early test flight. Note the instrumentation boom attached to the radome. (Grumman)

Studies for a dedicated electronic warfare aircraft based on the Intruder's airframe began in 1960 in response to a requirement issued by the Marine Corps. Originally designated the A2F-1H, the aircraft was to retain most of the attack capabilities of the A2F (later redesignated A-6A), while being optimized to serve as an airborne jamming platform. In order to accommodate the electronic equipment necessary to perform this mission, the nose section was lengthened by eight inches and the large "football" antenna fairing was added to the top of the vertical tail. This was the same fairing that would later be added to the Prowler and the EF-111A Raven.

Two additional pylons were added under the wings outboard of the fold mechanism. These were designed to carry the large ALQ-53 ECM reconnaissance pods, but only the first twelve aircraft were equipped with this system. The new pylons were designated stations A and B, leaving the original five stations numbered 1 through 5 as on the A-6A. When the ALQ-53 system was deleted, the new pylon stations remained and were used to carry chaff pods, Shrike missiles, or other stores. However, the subsequent ALQ-76 ECM pods could not be employed on these stations. It should also be noted that the addition of these outboard wing pylons meant that the speed

brakes at the wing tips were deleted, and the EA-6A retained the fuselage-mounted speed brakes long after they were deleted from other Intruder variants.

In 1962, a DOD standardization of designations did away with A2F-1H and replaced it with EA-6A. Officially the name of the aircraft remained Intruder, but it was more commonly referred to as the Electric Intruder.

The first prototype was built using the airframe of the eighth production A-6A, BuNo. 148618. Reconfigured as an EA-6A, this aircraft made its first flight on 16 April, 1963. This was followed by a second developmental aircraft which was designated NEA-6A. It was built from the airframe of the twenty-first A-6A, 149935, and it can be identified in photographs by the number 21 painted just below the "football."

The first twelve operational aircraft were all converted from A-6A airframes. These included BuNos. 147865, 148616, 148618, 149475, 149477, 149478, and 151595 through 151600. It was these aircraft that were fitted with the ALQ-53 systems and its teardrop-shaped pods that were carried on the new outer wing stations. The first of these was originally the second production A-6A, BuNo. 147865. As the oldest EA-6A airframe, it was nicknamed Methuselah, and this name remained with

As this EA-6A banks away from the camera, the extra pylon under each outer wing panel is clearly visible, as is one of the unusual hoop antennas under the wing tip. The addition of the extra pylon resulted in the elimination of the wing tip speed brakes. (Grumman)

The most common ECM pod seen on EA-6As was the ALQ-76. It is similar to the Prowler's ALQ-99 high band pod, but it is flat-sided with four panels on each side. At left is an ALQ-76 on a wing pylon, and at right is a rear view of another pod on the centerline station. Also note the ALQ-100 "chin-up bar" antenna on the pylon in the left photo. It was later deleted from EA-6As as it was from Prowlers.

the aircraft during its service with VMAQ-2 and VMCJ-3. Photographs of this aircraft appear on pages 60, 61, and 62. An additional fifteen Electric Intruders were built as EA-6As from the start, and these had Bureau numbers from 156979 through 156993. This brought the total EA-6A production to twenty-seven aircraft.

The ALQ-86 system replaced the ALQ-53, and this eliminated the latter's pods on the outboard pylons. However, the pylons remained to carry other stores.

In 1965, the ALQ-76 jamming pod was introduced, although it did not become completely operational for another three years. It was this pod that the EA-6A was most commonly associated with, and this manual jamming system proved effective during combat missions in Vietnam.

The EA-6A entered service with Marine composite squadrons, VMCJ-1, VMCJ-2, and VMCJ-3 during 1965, and VMCJ-1 was the first and only squadron to operate the aircraft in combat. The first missions in Vietnam were flown out of Da Nang AB during late 1966 in support of Navy and Marine alpha strikes. Later, while operating from Japan and the Philippines, VMCJ-1's EA-6As supported B-52s missions during Linebacker operations.

In 1975, Marine composite squadrons were eliminated. VMCJ-2 became VMAQ-2, and this squadron assumed the electronic warfare mission within Marine Corps aviation. EA-6As that were to remain in the inventory were transferred to VMAQ-2, and the rest were sent to Davis-Monthan AFB, Arizona, for storage. VMAQ-2 continued to operate these aircraft until they were re-

placed by EA-6B Prowlers in 1979.

But the replacement of the EA-6As with Prowlers in 1979 did not mean the end of service for the Electric Intruder. EA-6As that were transferred out of VMAQ-2, along with others taken out of storage at Davis-Monthan, found a new lease on life in three Navy squadrons that same year. The "Firebirds" of VAQ-33 became the only regular Navy squadron to operate the Electric Intruder except for a brief assignment with VX-5 for test and evaluation purposes. VAQ-33 used its EA-6As in the electronic warfare training role while acting as adversaries for Navy units during exercises.

The other two squadrons to receive EA-6As in 1979 were the Star Warriors of VAQ-209 and the Axemen of VAQ-309. These two units were the Navy Reserve squadrons for the Atlantic and Pacific Fleets respectively. In late 1981, VMAQ-4 became operational in EA-6As at NAS Whidbey Island, Washington.

The RECAP program was implemented in 1985 and involved eleven of the remaining EA-6As. This upgrade replaced the ALQ-100 system with the ALQ-126. EA-6As that went through RECAP can be identified by the addition of the "beer can" added to the aft end of the "football" fairing on the tail. This is the same feature added to Prowlers when the ALQ-126 was installed in EA-6Bs. Likewise, the "saw tooth" antenna fairing was also added to the base of the refueling probe.

VAQ-209, VAQ-309, and VMAQ-4 have since converted to EA-6B Prowlers. VAQ-33 was the last squadron to operate EA-6As, and these too have now been retired.

The "Firebirds" of VAQ-33 were an electronic warfare "adversary" squadron on the east coast. One of their EA-6As is shown here in the tactical paint scheme. See page 33 for a photograph of another one of the squadron's Electric Intruders in the gray over white scheme.

(Flightleader collection)

Navy Reserve squadrons also operated the EA-6A. At left is an aircraft from VAQ-209, while the Electric Intruder at right is in the markings of VAQ-309. These were the Naval Reserve squadrons for the Atlantic and Pacific fleets respectively. *(Both Grove via Flightleader)*

This photograph has been published before, but it is the only one known that shows the early EA-6A cockpit configuration as used in the first twelve aircraft with the ALQ-53 system. *(Grumman)*

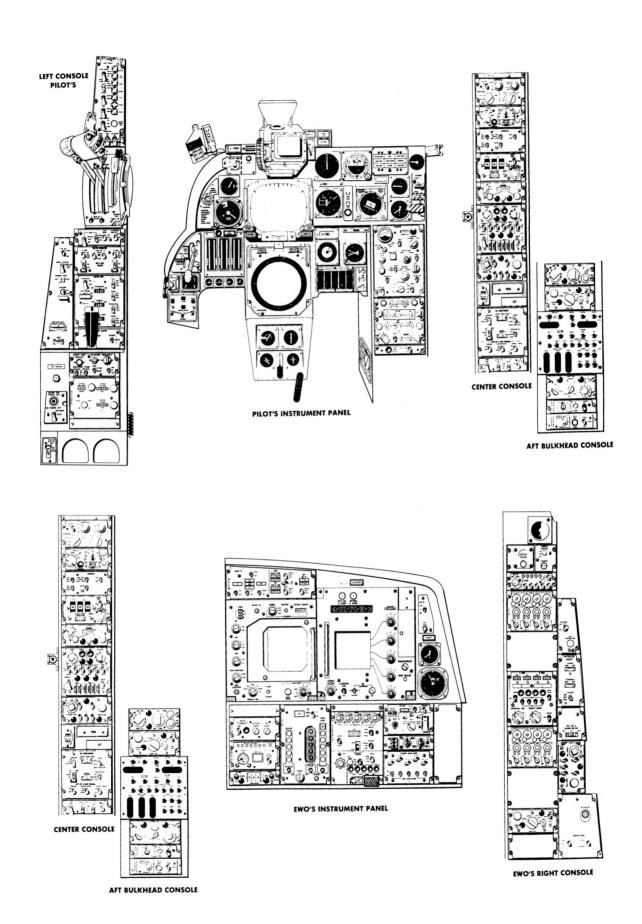

LEFT CONSOLE PILOT'S

PILOT'S INSTRUMENT PANEL

CENTER CONSOLE

AFT BULKHEAD CONSOLE

CENTER CONSOLE

AFT BULKHEAD CONSOLE

EWO'S INSTRUMENT PANEL

EWO'S RIGHT CONSOLE

The features of the later cockpit configuration used in the EA-6A are revealed in the drawings on this page.
(U. S. Navy)

EA-6A, 147865, METHUSELAH

The second production A-6A, 147865, became the first operational EA-6A and was accepted on 7 March, 1966. As the oldest EA-6A in the Navy, it was nicknamed Methuselah. On this page we take a look at this EA-6A in the markings of two units to which it was assigned. Then on the next two pages, is a pictorial "walkaround" showing some of the EA-6A's more important features. Methuselah is shown at left in the markings of VMAQ-2 flying over its home base of Cherry Point, North Carolina. The **OO** nose number indicates that it is assigned to the squadron commander. This photograph also shows the additional fence on the top of each wing.
(USMC photo)

The left side of 147865 is shown here while the aircraft was still assigned to VMAQ-2. Although it is impossible to see in this photograph, **METHUSELAH** is stencilled just forward and below the **OO** modex on the nose.
(Flightleader collection)

EA-6A, 147865, was later transferred to VMCJ-3. Note that an external fuel tank could be carried on the added outer wing pylon. Although the aircraft has been reassigned to a different unit, **METHUSELAH** remains on the nose just forward of and slightly below the **16**.
(Flightleader collection)

At left is a right side view of 147865, the day on which the following detailed photographs were taken. The unit designation **VMCJ-3** is stencilled on the fuselage above the wing instead of the more standard position further aft. At right is a close-up of the nose landing gear showing the large AN/ALQ-55 antenna on the forward nose gear door. Also note the landing/taxi light on the door. The lower anti-collision beacon is located further forward under the nose.

The left side of the nose section is shown here. Note the pitot probe on the top of the nose, and the small forward IFF/TACAN antenna located between it and the refueling probe. The name **METHUSELAH** can be seen stencilled on the side of the aircraft. The latch for the left forward equipment bay can be seen below the name.

A second pitot probe is on the right side of the upper nose section. Other features are basically the same as on standard Intruders, except that the EA-6A's nose is noticeably longer than that on the attack variants. The name **METHUSELAH** was painted in black on both sides of the aircraft as seen here.

Because the EA-6A did not have the speed brakes at the wing tips, the fuselage-mounted brakes were retained on the Electric Intruder even after they were deleted from other variants. The brakes were dark natural metal on the outside and gloss insignia red on the inside. The inside of the well was also gloss red.

The Doppler antenna fairing can be seen under the fuselage to the left in this photo. The large swept blade is the aft UHF communications antenna, and the smaller black blade is the aft IFF/TACAN antenna.

The EA-6A has the same tail cap radome as the EA-6B, but the antenna fairings on the sides of the vertical tail are not fitted. The "beer can" would later be added to the aft end of the "football" on the eleven EA-6As that went through the RECAP program.

MODELERS SECTION
KIT REVIEWS

Except for the Prowlers that come as part of the air wings for aircraft carrier kits, the smallest available model of the EA-6B is this 1/300th scale kit from Nichimo.

1/300th SCALE KIT

Nichimo EA-6B, Kit Number 20

Packaged with an F-4 Phantom, this is the smallest model of a Prowler that is available except for the ones that come as part of carrier air wings in models of aircraft carriers.

As might be expected, detailing is at a minimum in this tiny scale. There are no doors for the landing gear, no clear parts, and even the inboard wing pylons are missing. The outboard pylons come with low band ALQ-99 ECM pods already attached, and these same pylons have ALQ-100 antennas on their leading edges. A centerline pylon is provided, and it comes complete with an external fuel tank.

The canopies and windscreens are to be represented merely by painting them silver, pale blue, or whatever color the modeler thinks is appropriate. But black would not be a good choice, because the markings are for an aircraft from VMAQ-2 with a black hood around the cockpits. The aircraft has an all black vertical tail with a white rudder. The tail code is **CY**, and there is the famous *Playboy* bunny logo on the rudder.

For its size, this is not a bad little kit, but it would have been nice if inboard pylons and landing gear doors were included. We would like to see someone superdetail one of these little models, then build a 1/300th scale NIMITZ class carrier from scratch to display it on!

1/144th SCALE KITS

DML EA-6A, Kit Number 4544

Using their A-6E kit as a basis, DML added a new vertical tail with the appropriate "football" antenna fairing at the top and a pair of ECM pods to make this kit of an EA-6A. Also added were new outboard pylons with a Shrike missile for one and a Standard anti-radiation missile for the other. However, the instructions show these new pylons being placed where the inboard wing pylons should go. Be sure to put them in the correct positions outboard of the wing fold.

The ECM pods are ALQ-99 low band pods instead of the correct ALQ-76 pods used on the EA-6A. By filing the sides of the pods flat, they will become passable representations of the ALQ-76. They are also missing the ram

DML has the only model of the EA-6A in 1/144th scale. It is simply a modified version of their A-6E Intruder kits with the addition of a new vertical tail with the radome and two ALQ-76 ECM pods. The additional outboard pylons are also included with both Shrike and Standard anti-radiation missiles.

air turbine at the forward end, so this must be added from sprue or plastic rod. The vanes will be difficult to add in this small scale, and we recommend using tiny slivers of paper. The pods come attached to pylons which have the ALQ-100 antennas on the leading edge. The modeler should use the A-6E inboard wing pylons which come in this kit, but unfortunately there are no stores to go on them. There is only one external fuel tank, and that goes on the centerline station.

The cockpit area has DML's usual poor seats with even worse pilot figures. DML will greatly improve their 1/144th scale series of aircraft when they learn to eliminate these droid looking creatures from their ejection seats. There is no instrument panel, and this leaves a huge hole in the forward cockpit that is easily seen even through a closed canopy. Some thin plastic card should be cut to fit over this hole, and some details could be painted on to give a more realistic look.

Another problem is the opening for the engine inlets. These are too small and narrow, and their appearance will improve if they are opened up a little. The speed brakes and their fairings are present at the wing tips, so these must be removed. They were not present on the EA-6A. DML used the fuselage halves that come in their A-6 kits, so the nose is too short for an EA-6A. The UHF/ADF antenna fairing is missing from the spine, and the air conditioning and equipment cooling scoops are missing from the aft fuselage. These features can all be added from scratch without too much difficulty, but they should have been included in the kit. To their credit, DML did remember to include the additional fence for the top of each wing.

Fit around the inlets and exhausts will require some filling and sanding, but otherwise the model goes together without too much problem.

Decals are for an aircraft from VMAQ-2 in the light

gull gray over white scheme. The vertical tail is black, and the *Playboy* bunny logo is located on the white rudder. With a little time and patience, and with some simple corrective plastic surgery, a nice little model of the Electric Intruder can be built with this kit.

At press time for this book, the only 1/144th scale model of the Prowler was this kit from Revell of Germany. However, DML has announced that it will soon be releasing a Prowler kit in this, the smallest "standard" modeling scale.

Revell of Germany EA-6B, Kit Number 4055-0389

So far, this is the only Prowler kit that has been released in 1/144th scale. It is fairly accurate in shape, but lacks any wing fences. These should be added from thin plastic card. The engine inlets are far better than those found in DML's EA-6A kit covered above, and the pieces representing the forward end of the engines are provided to go inside each inlet. However, the exhausts are quite poor and will require some reshaping by the modeler. Fit is generally good except around the inlets, which seems to be a problem with all Intruder/Prowler kits. The fit of the canopies and windscreen is also quite bad. Whether they are shown open or closed, it will take a lot of work to get the canopies to look right. But the cockpit is quite nice for a 1/144th scale model and is devoid of any crew figures.

The biggest problem that we had with this kit was getting the soft plastic to stick together. It kept wanting to fall apart. After trying a variety of glues, we found that the thick gap-filler glues worked best. The four ECM pods are all the low band variety, but we filed the sides of one down so that it would represent a high band pod. We decided to use one high band pod and one low band pod on our model. The kit also comes with two external fuel tanks, so we placed these on the inboard wing pylons. Small pieces of sheet styrene can be used to make LAU-118 launchers, and AGM-88 HARM missiles can be obtained from LS Weapons Set Number 2. We added one HARM to the left outboard pylon of our review sample. These certainly dressed up the finished model. The forward nose landing gear door also had to be made from plastic card, because it was not included in the kit.

Decals are relatively sparse. Markings for a Prowler from VAQ-131 are provided, and although it is painted in the gray over white scheme, the markings are not colorful

at all. The second set of markings are for an aircraft from VAQ-139 in the tactical scheme.

The ALQ-100 antennas are present on the outer wing pylons, but it would be a simple task to change antenna patterns on this small model to make any Prowler upgrade that is desired.

DML EA-6B, Kit Number 4574

DML has announced the release of an EA-6B Prowler in 1/144th scale, and it is known that its kit number will be 4574. No other details of this kit were known at press time for this book.

1/72nd SCALE KITS

Fujimi EA-6A, Kit Number H-14

The most recent addition to Fujimi's family of Intruder kits is this model of the EA-6A. Although the box art indicates that this was a Desert Storm aircraft, no EA-6As were used in the Gulf War.

It seems that a number of model companies have not understood the difference between the ALQ-76 ECM pods used on the EA-6A and the different ALQ-99 pods used on Prowlers. Fujimi is guilty of making this mistake and has combined features from both types of pods in this kit. They correctly have the ALQ-76's four panels on each side, but they also have the slightly bulged keel of an ALQ-99. The bulge appears to be a bit too much for a high band pod, but not enough for a low band ALQ-99. But regardless, the correct ALQ-76 should have flat sides. (See page 57.) The plastic is too thin to file the sides flat, so some plastic surgery will be required to make the pods look right.

Otherwise, it appears that Fujimi got the EA-6A's features correct. A longer nose section is included, as are the pylons with the ALQ-100 antennas. The extra fences are provided for the tops of the wings, and the additional pylons are included to be mounted outboard of the wing fold. Unfortunately, there are no stores to go on them. The wings are the same as included in Fujimi's other Intruder kits, but the instructions do state that the hinges

The only 1/72nd scale model of the EA-6A is from Fujimi and was issued as part of their "family" of Intruder kits. It is an excellent model except that it has ALQ-99 ECM pods instead of the correct ALQ-76 pods. Contrary to what the box art says, EA-6As were not used in Operation Desert Storm.

for the wing tip speed brakes should be removed.

It is evident that the fuselage halves are different than what is provided in Fujimi's basic Intruder kits, because the vertical tail and "football" are all molded as part of the fuselage pieces. The UHF/ADF antenna fairing and the additional scoops are provided for the spine and aft fuselage. Even the inhibitor plate at the bottom of the rudder is a small separate piece that glues nicely into place. The speed brakes on the fuselage are separate pieces that can be shown open or closed. However, it will be necessary to drill out the holes in each of the brakes.

Because of complex curves in the design, all Intruder and Prowler kits suffer from some fit problems, and this is no exception. But if care is taken during assembly, these problems will be minimal and rather easily solved.

Fujimi did an excellent job of providing interiors for the engine inlets, and the S-shaped exhaust pipes are included. This means that when you look into the inlets, you don't see where the boarding steps are molded into its side. In this age of hi-tech scale modeling, it is surprising that more model companies do not provide interiors for the inlets and exhausts. There is equally nice detailing in the cockpit with raised features on the instrument panel and consoles. If the modeler does not want to spend the time with the raised detail, an option is provided in the form of decals as well. We hope other model companies are taking notice!!

The slats can be shown in the extended position, and the landing gear and wheel wells are also nicely done. Even the decal sheet is excellent with options for four different aircraft. Markings for colorful EA-6As from VMAQ-2, VAQ-209, and VAQ-309 are provided, and these are to be applied on the gray over white scheme. The fourth aircraft on the decal sheet is in the tactical scheme and is for an aircraft from VMAQ-2.

Overall, this is an excellent kit, with the ECM pods being the only glaring error. It is the only EA-6A presently available in 1/72nd scale, but fortunately it is a good one. We rate it as the best EA-6A in any scale.

Hobbycraft EA-6B, Kit Number HC1337

First, it is important to note that this was one of the original kits released by Hobbycraft, and it should not be confused or compared with any of their more recent issues. The kit is very similar to the Hasegawa kit, but is not nearly as well done.

The cockpit assembly consists of a tub, four seats, front and rear instrument panels, a control column, and the actuators for the canopies. The seats don't resemble the real thing, and should be replaced. Seats used in F-14 kits and after-market F-14 seats can be considered as alternatives. There is raised detailing in the cockpit tub, but this is not accurate. Although the kit instructions indicate that there are decals for the front and rear instrument panels, none are provided on the decal sheet.

The wing assemblies consist of top and bottom halves. An examination of these reveals that the airfoil section is incorrect, being too thin and not blunt enough on the leading edges.

Assembly of the fuselage, cockpit, and inlets is straight forward. However, there are major fit problems in these areas that will take a lot of filling and sanding.

Alan Toon updated the 1/72nd scale Hobbycraft kit to build this model of a Block 86 Prowler. The Hobbycraft kit falls short of the Hasegawa model when it comes to accuracy and detailing.

The radome is of a different size and shape from the fuselage, so again a lot of filling and sanding will be required to achieve the proper contours. The inlets and exhausts have similar fit problems. Like the Hasegawa kit, the area where the tail hook is glued to the fuselage is hollow. Once the tail hook is in place, you can still see up into the aft fuselage. Some plastic card is needed to correct this problem.

Care must be taken in adding the wings and horizontal stabilizers to the fuselage in order to get things lined up correctly. Once the glue has set, the filling and sanding begins again because of the poor fit. External stores consist of five ECM pods and three drop tanks.

The clear parts are on the thick side, and there is no gold tinting on the canopies. This can be added by using thin Gunze-Sangyo clear yellow on the insides.

Decals include markings for an aircraft from VAQ-132 and another from VAQ-139. Both are painted in the tactical scheme. The kit-supplied decals are not suitable for the serious scale modeler, so it is best to use after-market decals instead.

In summary, this kit can be built into a nice model with enough work, but the Hasegawa Prowler is much better and worth the difference in price.

Review by Alan Toon

Hasegawa EA-6B, Various Kit Numbers

Clearly the best of the 1/72nd scale Prowlers, this kit was first issued in the United States when Minicraft was the importer for Hasegawa models. The first release was kit number 1137, and it came with Scale-Master decals for an aircraft from VAQ-130 in the gray over white scheme. From the first, the kit offered both the early in-flight refueling probe as well as the later one with the ALQ-126 receiver antenna at its base. The other ALQ-126 antenna, better known as the "beer can," was an option that could be added to the base of the aft end of the "football" fairing if appropriate for the particular aircraft the modeler was building.

Five accurate ALQ-99 ECM pods were provided, four of which were high band pods with the remaining one being a low band pod. Those that were supposed to go

Easily the best Prowler kit in any scale is the 1/72nd scale model from Hasegawa. It has been released a number of times with minor improvements and updates. This model was built by Clyde Mills shortly after the kit was first released in the United States by Minicraft.

on the wing pylons had the proper wedge-shaped spacer molded on to the top of the pod. Three external fuel tanks were also included that could be substituted for the pods as desired. The outboard pylons have the ALQ-100 antennas molded on to their leading edges. In later issues, two sets of outboard pylons were included; one with these antennas and one without.

The canopies were tinted as they should be, but so was the windscreen. There is no tinting on the Prowler's windscreen, so this part should have been left clear. Beneath the canopies, the cockpits had detailing that was about average for kits issued in the late 1970s and early 1980s. Although there was some raised detailing on the consoles, it was not really accurate, and decals were provided for the two instrument panels. The ejection seats left a lot to be desired, and unfortunately, they have not been improved on any subsequent releases. We suggest modifying Verlinden 1/72nd scale F-14 seats for use in this kit. They will go a long way in improving the appearance of the model if the canopies remain open.

There is no detailing to speak of in the wheel wells, but the struts and wheels are well represented. The fairings at the leading edge of each wing root are not entirely accurate, and they do not extend back on to the forward main gear doors as they should. But this can easily be corrected with a little scrap plastic.

A real problem is that there is no well for the tail hook, and when assembled, you can look past the tail hook up into the hollow aft fuselage. Time should be taken to add a well with plastic card.

The engine inlets do not have the small step on top of them as they should, but this is easily added. However, the fold-down steps on either side of the forward fuselage are present and may be shown in the opened or closed position. The fold-out steps in each inlet are also separate pieces that can be displayed open or closed. The problem is that you can look in the front of the inlet and see a flat face that has a hole where the steps are supposed to fit. Filling this is a problem. It would have been far better if Hasegawa had provided interiors for the inlets as Fujimi did.

Scribing is of the raised variety, but it is nicely done, being both accurate and petite. Hasegawa correctly represented the wing fold fairings on top of the wings as well as the fences and the stiffener next to the walkway.

Fit problems exist, but as Intruder/Prowler kits go, this one is the best of the group. Care should be taken around the intakes and exhausts to minimize the amount of filling and sanding that is required.

Kit K14 was the same as 1137 except for the box art and decals, but it was issued by Hasegawa, and not by Minicraft. Markings included Prowlers from VAQ-131 and VAQ-134 in the gray over white scheme.

In kit K14X, there were small changes in the plastic. The fairing at the base of the rudder was made larger and less tapered, and the antenna pattern on the spine was changed to reflect the ICAP-2 configuration. The clear parts were left untinted, meaning that the modeler could tint the canopies as desired while leaving the windscreen clear. Decals provided markings for aircraft from VMAQ-2 and VAQ-136, both of which were in the gray over white scheme.

The most recent release of this kit to date is kit number SP105. The tinted canopies and windscreen have reappeared, but otherwise the plastic remains as it was in K14X. Additional instructions tell the modeler to remove the ALQ-92 antenna from under the nose and the doppler antenna from under the aft fuselage in order to build a later ICAP-2 aircraft. However, they fail to point out that the air scoop on the aft left fuselage should also be removed, because it was also part of the ALQ-92 system. Two sets of outboard wing pylons are included; one set with the ALQ-100 antennas and one without. Be sure to use the ones without these antennas when building a model of any ICAP-1 or later aircraft. By changing the antenna patterns on the spine and lower aft fuselage of this model, it would be simple to update this kit to a Block 86 or Block 89 aircraft.

Markings with this release include an aircraft from VMAQ-2 and another from VAQ-135, both of which are in the tactical paint scheme. A second decal sheet adds two more Prowlers, and these are both Gulf War veterans from VAQ-136.

Without a doubt, this is the most accurate model of the Prowler available in any scale, but it does have some areas that can use a little detailing. By paying close attention to the differences between the various Prowler upgrades as explained and illustrated in this book, the modeler can easily build this kit into an accurate scale model of any Prowler variant.

The Matchbox EA-6B is the least desirable of all 1/72nd scale Prowlers. This is not a kit to be considered by serious scale modelers.

Matchbox EA-6B, Kit Number PK-410

Simply stated, this kit is crude when compared to the Hasegawa and even the Hobbycraft Prowlers in 1/72nd scale. It is molded in olive green and white plastic and has very heavy panel lines as found on so many Matchbox kits. It lacks detail in the interior and wheel wells, and the landing gear is poorly executed. Although Matchbox designed the kit so that the wings could be folded, the resulting exposed hinge mechanism does not come close to representing the real thing.

Four ECM pods are provided, and they are supposed to represent ALQ-99 low band pods. They lack any surface detailing whatsoever. The clear parts are only fair, but the canopies are not tinted, and the framing on the windscreen is too thick.

The decal sheet provides markings for Prowlers from VAQ-130, VAQ-132, and VAQ-135. All are early EA-6Bs that are painted in the gray over white scheme.

Suffice it to say that this is not a kit that can be considered for use by the serious scale modeler. Enough said!

1/48th SCALE KITS

Airfix & MPC EA-6B, Different Kit Numbers

This older kit of an ICAP-1 Prowler is not nearly up to the standards of the newer Monogram kit, even though it features some items not included on the later kit. The fairings on the main landing gear doors are closer representations of the real thing, the ECM pods have the proper wedged-shaped spacer that go between them and the wing pylons, the vanes on the ram air turbines are correctly angled, and the wing fold mechanism is more accurate than in the Monogram kit. The problem is that although Airfix/MPC included these pieces, the execution is so poor as to make them unusable even in correcting the inaccuracies of the Monogram kit.

The overall shape and raised panel lines are basically correct for an ICAP-1 or earlier Prowler. The raised detailing in the cockpit is easily dry brushed to achieve a nice effect. But the seats and the pilot figures leave a lot to be desired. There is almost no detailing in the wheel wells, and there are some sink holes in some locations that are hard to get at. But the worst problem is the fit. Any modeler who attempts to build this kit should be prepared to spend a lot of time filling and sanding. The worst area is the engine inlets as it is on most Intruder and Prowler kits.

The canopies are tinted as they should be, but so is the windscreen which should not have any tint. All four of the ECM pods are of the low band variety, and two fuel tanks are also included. The decal sheet in the MPC release is nice, and provides markings for an aircraft from VAQ-136 in the gray over white paint scheme. We were unable to locate an original Airfix release of this kit, so we do not know if this is the same decal sheet that was also included in that release.

In short, the level of effort required to make this kit into a reasonable model is just too great to make it worthwhile except for the most dedicated Airfix/MPC fans.

Bobby Winnett and Jim Rotramel contributed to this review.

It required Bobby Winnett many hours of work to turn the crude Airfix 1/48th scale kit into this excellent model of a Prowler from VAQ-135 that was used on the raids against Libya. (Holmes)

Revell's 1/48th scale EA-6A was used by Joe Driver, Jr. to build this model of an Electric Intruder from VMAQ-2.

Revell EA-6A, Kit Number 4401

Following closely on the heels of the Revell A-6E Intruder was this kit of the EA-6A. The differences between this kit and the earlier A-6E release include a new fuselage with an extended nose at one end and the "football" antenna at the other. The wings are different in that the speed brake actuators and the RHAW antennas were removed. The external stores were changed from bombs to jamming pods, a chaff pod, and Shrike anti-radiation missiles. The instrument panel was also changed to more closely represent that found in the EA-6A. All other parts are the same in both kits.

The cockpit has raised detailing on both the instrument panel and side consoles, and this detailing is fairly accurate. The only major item that is missing is the circuit breaker panel between the seats. A separate piece for the throttle quadrants would have also improved an otherwise nice cockpit. The ejection seats consist of the seat backs that are attached to seat bottoms which are part of the cockpit tub. This is typical for Revell-Monogram, and it is something they need to get away from. Ejection seats should be separate pieces that can be installed when completely assembled. This would make detailing the seats easier for both the manufacturer and the modeler, and it would also allow for easy substitution of after-market seats if desired. The area behind the seats is also nicely done. When fitting the cockpit tub to the fuselage halves, it is recommended that it be reinforced under the side consoles to insure a snug fit.

Assembling the wings will take a lot of time, patience, and effort. First of all, the trailing edges of the wing are too thick and should be thinned down. On the leading edges of the wings are two protrusions. Remove these and mark their place prior to lining up the wings and sanding the seams. Reattach them when the sanding is complete. The wing halves do not fit well so they will need some coaxing. The wing tips are completely inaccurate, being too square in shape. They must be rounded to the correct shape, but be careful not to reduce the span of the wings, because it is correct.

But the problems do not stop here. When assembling the wings to the fuselage, shims must be added at the leading edge fillet and at the exhausts to get everything to line up correctly. It would have been better if the exhaust area had been molded as a separate piece. This would have allowed for easier construction and eliminated the poor fit.

Another item to be aware of concerns the thickness of the wing in relation to the fuselage area where it attaches. During construction of the review sample, one wing had to be compressed and the other had to be expanded to fit properly. When gluing the wing to the fuselage, the modeler must hold the parts together until the glue sets up, otherwise the wing will push itself free.

The intakes do not have the proper curvature on the top. They are too flat, so some reshaping must be done here. Also, they are not deep enough. As a result, the turbine fan blades are too far forward and are too small as well. Fit is not good inside or outside the inlets, so be prepared for more filling and sanding.

The part that forms the underside of the fuselage has little scoops molded on it. These should have been separate pieces, because molding them as part of the underside of the fuselage meant that they had to be skewed sideways in order for the part to release from the mold. These scoops will require a lot or reworking to make them look right. In some cases it may be better to remove them and make new ones from scratch. The sides of the nose gear well are best painted and attached to this center piece prior to fitting it to the fuselage. The nose gear doors would have best been left off as separate pieces, because they block off the area around the inlets and make sanding difficult.

The worst fitting part in this kit is the windscreen. The instrument panel coaming must already be in place, or the windscreen will not come close to fitting properly. Also, the in-flight refueling probe must be removed in order to get the windscreen attached, filled, and sanded. Once the windscreen is attached, a considerable amount of filling is required. The canopy has the correct bubble cross-section but is difficult to glue into place. The canopy actuator makes for a difficult fit by forcing the rear of the canopy up when placed in the open position. Also, there is no overhead console for the canopy even though this is a noticeable item on the real thing.

There are no pins or holes provided for the pitot

probes, so just eyeball them to the correct placement on the anti-glare panel forward of the windscreen. The lower anti-collision light, that attaches to the bottom of the nose, needs to have its placement divot cleaned out before attaching it or it will lean to one side.

The landing gear struts suffer from too much detail molded into one piece. It is nice that Revell wanted to represent all of the brake lines, but the pieces suffer from poor mold alignment. It is best to strip down the parts to the essential minimum, then add the details. The retraction arms for both main gear are mislabled on the instruction sheet and should be used on the opposite side from what is indicated for proper fit. The main landing gear parts do not have a sturdy attachment to the wing, and they are difficult to align. The nose strut, although accurate, is very busy and difficult to clean up. The forward main landing gear doors do include the actuator, and this is nicely done. The wheel well detail is fair, but could use some extra work.

One thing not mentioned on the instructions is the beacon light behind the canopy, however the part is provided in the kit. The ALQ-76 ECM pods are too long, and the nose of each pod has the wrong shape. Although the EA-6A did not have the wedge-shaped spacers between the pods and the pylons like the Prowler, the pods were still mounted at a noticeable nose down angle. This can be seen in the photograph on page 57. Shrike anti-radiation missiles are also included.

The kit provides three blade antennas, which is short by at least one. Antenna patterns varied from aircraft to aircraft, so check the photographs of the EA-6A being modeled to determine size, shape, and location.

Decals are provided for two EA-6As. One is from VAQ-209 and is painted in the gray over white scheme, while the second is in the tactical scheme with markings for VAQ-309.

Overall, this is a good representation of the EA-6A, and the model looks impressive when completed. Shape and outline are basically correct as are most of the details. But building it is frustrating due to the multitude of fit problems. A few more pieces should have been included such as the overhead console in the canopy, separate scoops under the aircraft, and a separate tail hook that would have been easier to paint. Complete and separate ejection seats would also have been nice. If the modeler takes his time with the fit problems and reworks some parts, a very nice model awaits at the end of a rough and bumpy road.

Review by Joe Driver, Jr.

Monogram EA-6B, Kit Number 5611

This kit represents an ICAP-1 Prowler, and it looks great in the box. It has very nice cockpit and landing gear detail when compared to the much older Airfix/MPC kit. The outline is also correct, and this contributes to the illusion of perfection. However, it suffers from poor research which makes building it a frustrating experience--even if it didn't have some moderate fit problems. The major errors each require some discussion as to what they are and how they must be corrected.

The wing fold mechanism as represented in the kit is

Monogram's 1/48th scale Prowler is nicely molded, but it suffers from poor research. It has several features found on the Intruder but not on the Prowler. The wings are incorrect at the tip, wing fold, and root. The Intruder's armor is present, but it should have been deleted, and the ECM pods are inaccurate. However, it still rates better than the Airfix/MPC kit.

the one found on Intruders with the original metal wings. This is because Monogram put their Intruder's wing on the Prowler, and this is not correct. The Prowler's wing is different at the root, top, fold, and underneath. The wing fold on the Prowler is completely different than what Monogram has provided, so this area must be totally rebuilt from scratch. See page 51 in this book for detailed photographs of the wing fold area. On top of the wing, the EA-6B wing fold features a large fairing with two hinged covers. The fairing is much wider than that found on Intruders with metal wings.

The Prowler's wing fairings in front of the main landing gear doors are smaller than those found on the Intruder, with the former's flaps extending about eight inches farther inboard. Unfortunately, the kit uses the Intruder's fairing, so the whole area around the main landing gear must be rebuilt. As part of this mistake, the fairings on the forward main gear doors are also missing.

The high band ALQ-99 ECM pods were taken from Revell's EA-6A kit. These are actually ALQ-76 pods which lack the slightly bulged keel of the newer pods. The two high band pods are seven scale inches too long, while the single low band pod is fourteen scale inches too short. It is also located eighteen scale inches too far forward. Each of the real pods are 190-inches long. Although the low band pod is bulged, it was done in a crude and inaccurate manner. The vanes on the ram air turbines at the forward end of the pods are oriented almost ninety degrees from their "on the ground" position. The wedge-shaped spacers that go between each wing pylon and the ECM pods are missing from the kit.

Most of the antennas are incorrectly shaped. Only parts 59, 113, and 123 can be used as molded. Also, there is no information indicating how to accurately locate any of the antennas.

Every scoop to be added to the kit, and most of the ones molded onto it, are the wrong size and shape. Locating information is also incorrect. For example, the fuel vent scoop is located on the right side of the fuselage in the drawings, but on the left side in the scribing on the kit. The drawings have the correct side, but the wrong location.

The kit features the same armor plating found on the Intruder, but this plating is not present on the Prowler. The raised areas on the flanks of the engines, under the wings, and under the tail must all be removed.

The prominent air conditioning exhaust vent, located on the right fuselage just aft of the engine nozzle, was omitted from the kit. The fairings above the fuel dump vents near the tips of each wing were also left off. The total temperature probe is missing from the left inlet, and the angle of attack probe is missing from the right inlet. These certainly should be included on a 1/48th scale model.

The external stiffeners next to the anti-skid walkway on top of the wings are the wrong size and shape, and they are located in the incorrect place.

The refueling probe is angled over in front of the pilot's side, however it should be angled to the ECMO-1's side by twelve degrees.

The model is nicely molded, and has some good detailing. Both clear and tinted canopies and windscreens are provided, so the modeler should choose the clear windscreen and tinted canopies. Decals are for a Prowler from VAQ-131 in the gray over white scheme with colorful markings.

Although the poor research resulted in quite a few important errors in this kit, there is really nothing about it that makes this kit unbuildable. By carefully correcting each of the errors, an excellent model can be built. These corrections will be simpler if the modeler waits for the release of the kit from Cutting Edge Modelworks covered below, but they can also be accomplished from scratch by a competent modeler. This Monogram model is far better than the older Airfix/MPC kit, and it is the place to start for anyone who wants to build an EA-6B in 1/48th scale.

Review by Jim Rotramel

CONVERSION KITS & ACCESSORIES

<u>Airmodel EA-6A & EA-6B Conversion Kit Number 326</u>

Prior to the release of Hasegawa's Prowler and Fujimi's EA-6A, using this kit was the only way to build these aircraft in 1/72nd scale. Various antennas, ECM pods, canopies, and other parts were provided to build both the EA-6A and the EA-6B, and the instructions were excellent and well detailed for a conversion kit that came out in the early 1970s. The kit was intended to be used with the Frog/Hasegawa 1/72nd scale A-6A, and with work, a respectable model could be constructed. But with Hasegawa's nice Prowler kit and Fujimi's excellent EA-6A, there is no more need for a modeler to do all of this work.

The author used the Airmodel conversion kit and a Hasegawa 1/72nd scale A-6A Intruder to build this model of an EA-6A from VMCJ-1. This model was built before the Fujimi 1/72nd scale EA-6A became available.

<u>Maquettes Dauzie EA-6A & KA-6D Conversion Kit Number 72 004</u>

Also released long before Fujimi's EA-6A and KA-6D, this 1/72nd scale resin kit provided parts to convert the Hasegawa A-6A to an EA-6A or KA-6D. The only part for the tanker was the drogue refueling hose assembly to go under the aft fuselage. For the EA-6A, this kit included a longer radome, the AN/ALQ-55 antenna for the forward nose gear door, a UHF/ADF fairing for the spine, the additional intake scoops for the aft fuselage, and, of course, the "football" fairing for the tail. Two ECM pods were also included, but these were low band ALQ-99s, not the correct ALQ-76 pods used with the EA-6A. The ram air turbines that were to be glued to the forward end of these two pods had a lot of flash that had to be removed very carefully.

This is the Maquettes Dauzie EA-6A & KA-6D conversion kit in 1/72nd scale. The resin parts were nicely molded, except that there was a lot of flash on the two ram air turbines that went on the ECM pods. The pods themselves were ALQ-99 low band pods instead of being the correct ALQ-76 pods used on the EA-6A.

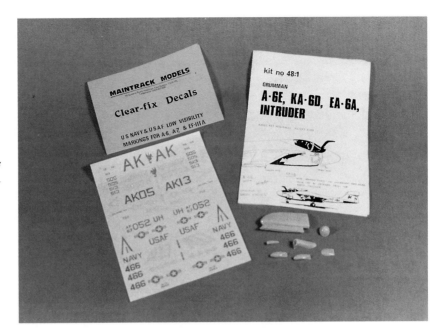

Maintrack Models kit number 48-1 contained parts to convert the Fujimi 1/48th scale A-6A into an A-6E, KA-6D, or EA-6A.

Maintrack Models Intruder Conversion Kit Number 48-1

This kit provides plastic parts to convert the Fujimi 1/48th scale A-6A into an A-6E, KA-6D, or EA-6A. The "football" fairing for the top of the vertical tail is included as are the required additional air scoops. The UHF/ADF antenna fairing for the spine is the other EA-6A part that is provided.

Dry transfer decals come with the kit, but these are for an A-6, A-7, and an EF-111. None appear to be appropriate for the EA-6A.

The plastic parts provided in this kit are well done, and a modeler may want to use the refueling basket to make a KA-6D. However, now that Revell's EA-6A has been released in 1/48th scale, this kit is of less value than before. To do a correct conversion, the modeler would have to make more changes to an A-6A kit than just adding the parts provided in this conversion kit. The most difficult change would be to lengthen the nose section.

True Details Kit Number 26020

This photoetched metal kit provides instrument panels to upgrade the Monogram 1/48th scale Prowler to an ICAP-2 version. Handles and buckles are included for the seats, but the survival kit buckles are much too large and shouldn't be used. Also provided are the formation light panels that go on each side of the fuselage. This kit is certainly worthwhile in upgrading the Monogram EA-6B.

Leading Edge Modelworks EA-6B Kit

Leading Edge Modelworks has announced plans to release a kit for the Monogram 1/48th scale Prowler that will correct all of the major mistakes that Monogram made. At press time for this book, no information had been made available as to kit number or release date, but whenever this kit becomes available, it will be extremely helpful to anyone wishing to build the Monogram kit into an accurate Prowler.

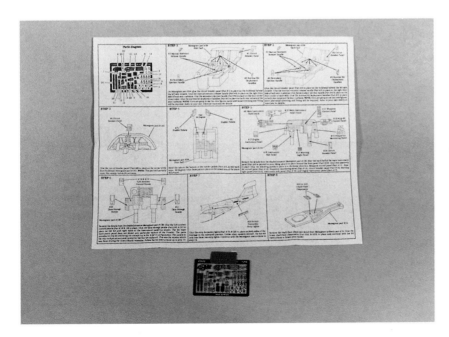

True Details makes this photoetched metal detail set for the Monogram 1/48th scale Prowler kit. It has parts for an ICAP-2 cockpit and also provides formation panel lights for the aft fuselage.

DECAL LISTING

MANUFACTURER & SHEET NUMBER	SCALE	TYPE	BUREAU NUMBER	UNIT	TAIL CODE	MODEX	SCHEME	COMMENTS
Scale-Master SM-16	1/72nd	EA-6B	158649	VAQ-131	NH	621	gray over white	Refueling probe should be bent to left when viewed from the front, not to the right as shown on the instructions.
SuperScale 72-079	1/72nd	EA-6A	156989	VMCJ-1	RM	2	gray over white	
		EA-6A	149475	VMCJ-2	CY	22	gray over white	*Playboy* bunny logo on rudder
SuperScale 72-225	1/72nd	EA-6B	159584	VAQ-132	NG	623	gray over white	USS CONSTELLATION
		EA-6B	158650	VAQ-136	AG	617	gray over white	USS INDEPENDENCE
		EA-6B	158810	VAQ-137	AE	700	gray over white	USS AMERICA
		EA-6B	158040	VAQ-129	TR	04	gray over white	
SuperScale 72-226	1/72nd	EA-6B	160707	VMAQ-2	CY	624	gray over white	*Playboy* bunny logo on black tail with white rudder
		EA-6B	158040	VAQ-135	NE	623	gray over white	
		EA-6B	159909	VAQ-135	AJ	611	gray over white	USS NIMITZ
		EA-6B	158802	VAQ-133	AJ	611	gray over white	USS AMERICA
SuperScale 72-299	1/72nd	EA-6B	159586	VAQ-138	AC	606	gray over white	USS SARATOGA
SuperScale 72-428	1/72nd	EA-6A	156992	VMCJ-2	AA	612	gray over white	USS FORRESTAL; *Playboy* bunny logo on rudder
SuperScale 72-532	1/72nd	EA-6B	161242	VAQ-132	AG	606	tactical	USS DWIGHT D. EISENHOWER; no unit designation on fuselage
		EA-6B	158029	VAQ-135	AB	604	tactical	No unit designatioin on fuselage
		EA-6B	158801	VAQ-137	AC	05	tactical	
SuperScale 72-533	1/72nd	EA-6B	158040	VAQ-134	NL	604	tactical	USS CARL VINSON
		EA-6B	161774	VAQ-139	NK	605	tactical	USS CONSTELLATION; no unit designation on fuselage
		EA-6B	160435	VMAQ-2	CY	06	tactical	no unit designation on fuselage
SuperScale 72-620	1/72nd	EA-6B	158034	VAQ-139	NK	606	tactical	USS INDEPENDENCE; No painting instructions, and tail markings are incomplete and in error. **606** is missing from both sides of rudder. **CAG** and **DCAG** on "football" are too large.
SuperScale 72-648	1/72nd	EA-6B	163525	VAQ-131	NE	606	tactical	USS RANGER; Desert Storm
		EA-6B	163527	VAQ-141	AJ	621	tactical	USS THEODORE ROOSEVELT; Desert Storm; *Eve of Destruction* nose art
		EA-6B	161348	VAQ-137	AB	622	tactical	USS AMERICA; Desert Storm
SuperScale 48-009	1/48th	EA-6A	156992	VMCJ-2	AA	612	gray over white	USS FORRESTAL; *Playboy* bunny logo on rudder
SuperScale 48-153	1/48th	EA-6B	159584	VAQ-132	NG	623	gray over white	USS CONSTELLATION
		EA-6B	158810	VAQ-137	AE	700	gray over white	USS AMERICA
SuperScale 48-154	1/48th	EA-6B	160707	VMAQ-2	CY	624	gray over white	*Playboy* bunny logo on black tail with white rudder
		EA-6B	159909	VAQ-135	AJ	611	gray over white	
SuperScale 48-203	1/48th	EA-6B	158650	VAQ-136	AG	617	gray over white	USS INDEPENDENCE
		EA-6B	158040	VAQ-129	TR	04	gray over white	
SuperScale 48-204	1/48th	EA-6B	158802	VAQ-133	AJ	611	gray over white	USS AMERICA
		EA-6B	158040	VAQ-135	NE	623	gray over white	
SuperScale 48-307	1/48th	EA-6B	161242	VAQ-132	AG	606	tactical	USS DWIGHT D. EISENHOWER; no unit designation on fuselage
		EA-6B	158029	VAQ-135	AB	604	tactical	no unit designation on fuselage
		EA-6B	158801	VAQ-137	AC	05	tactical	
SuperScale 48-308	1/48th	EA-6B	158040	VAQ-134	NL	604	tactical	USS CARL VINSON
		EA-6B	161774	VAQ-139	NK	605	tactical	USS CONSTELLATION; no unit designation on fuselage
		EA-6B	160435	VMAQ-2	CY	06	tactical	no unit designation on fuselage
SuperScale 48-369	1/48th	EA-6A	156989	VMCJ-1	RM	2	gray over white	
		EA-6A	156992	VMCJ-2	AA	612	gray over white	USS FORRESTAL; same as on sheet 48-009
		EA-6A	149487	VMCJ-2	CY	22	gray over white	*Playboy* bunny logo on tail
SuperScale 48-404	1/48th	EA-6B	158034	VAQ-139	NK	606	tactical	USS INDEPENDENCE; No painting instructions, and tail markings are incomplete and in error. **606** is missing from both sides of rudder. **CAG** and **DCAG** on "football" are too large.
SuperScale 48-436	1/48th	EA-6B	163525	VAQ-131	NE	606	tactical	USS RANGER; Desert Storm
		EA-6B	163527	VAQ-141	AJ	621	tactical	USS THEODORE TOOSEVELT: Desert Storm; *Eve of Destruction* nose art
		EA-6B	161348	VAQ-137	AB	622	tactical	USS AMERICA; Desert Storm

NOTE: This listing includes available after-market decal sheets for the EA-6A and EA-6B kits as of September 1994, which was press time for this book. No after-market sheets for the EA-6A or EA-6B had been released in 1/144th scale at this time.